One World One Earth

*Educating Children
for Social Responsibility*

One World One Earth

*Educating Children
for Social Responsibility*

Merryl Hammond and Rob Collins

New Society Publishers

Gabriola Island, BC   Philadelphia, PA

Canadian Cataloguing in Publication Data

Hammond, Merryl.
One world, one earth

Includes bibliographical references.
ISBN 1-55092-188-6 (bound). — 1-55092-189-4 (pbk.)

1. International education. 2. Responsibility — Social aspects — Study and teaching. 3. Social justice — Study and teaching. 4. Peace — Study and teaching. 5. Environmental education. I. Collins, Rob. II. Title.

LC 1090.H34 1992   370.11'5   C92-091409-8

Inquiries regarding requests to reprint all or part of *One World, One Earth: Educating Children for Social Responsibility* should be addressed to:
New Society Publishers
P.O. Box 189, Gabriola Island, BC V0R 1X0, or
4527 Springfield Avenue, Philadelphia, PA 19143

Hardcover   ISBN CAN 1-55092-188-6   ISBN USA 0-86571-246-8
Paperback   ISBN CAN 1-55092-189-4   ISBN USA 0-86571-247-6

Printed in the United States of America on partially recycled paper by Capital City Press of Montpelier, Vermont.

Cover design by g.e. jarrett.
Book typeset by Consultancy for Alternative Education of Montréal, Québec.

To order directly from the publisher, add $2.50 to the price for the first copy, 75¢ each additional copy (plus GST in Canada). Send check or money order to:
New Society Publishers
P.O. Box 189, Gabriola Island, BC V0R 1X0, *or in the U.S.A.,*
4527 Springfield Avenue, Philadelphia, PA 19143

New Society Publishers is a project of the New Society Educational Foundation, a nonprofit, tax-exempt, public foundation in the United States, and of the Catalyst Education Society, a non-profit society in Canada. Opinions expressed in this book do not necessarily represent positions of the New Society Educational Foundation, nor the Catalyst Education Society.

Contents

Foreword *by Dr. Rosalie Bertell* vii

Acknowledgments ix

Preface xi

Chapter 1 Raising Issues, Raising Consciousness: Learning Activities   **1**

Choosing Appropriate Learning Activities 3

Reading 4

Composing and Writing 5

Art and Craftwork 10

Cooperative Games 11

Using Our Bodies 14

Dramatic Work 17

Music 18

Food, Cooking, and Eating 19

Simulations and Simulation Games 20

Research Projects 21

Visits and Visitors 22

Taking Action 22

Chapter 2 Discussion Starters   **24**

Role-plays 25

Skits 26

Testimonials 27

Graphics 27

Stories, Poems, Songs, and Chants 32

Movies, Videos, and Slides 33

Other Visual and Audio Aids 34

Questions 35

Brainstorming 35

Quotations 36

Chapter 3   Ice Breaking and Community Building   37

Breaking the Ice 37

Ice Breakers to Introduce Participants 38

Setting the Scene for a New Topic or Theme 41

Energizing Participants 42

Community Building 42

Building a Cooperative Learning Community 45

Chapter 4   Session Plans   49

Planning a Provisional Program 49

Environmental Education: I Am a Child of the Earth 56

International Education: I Am a Member of the World Family 64

Orientation Session for Day Camp Staff 64

International Sessions for Children 69

Peace Education: I Will Work for Peace 75

Special Events and Ceremonies 82

Chapter 5   Getting Organized   90

Working with Family Members 90

Working in a Community Setting 93

Working in an Institutional Setting 96

Generating and Sustaining Enthusiasm 101

Creating a Ripple Effect: Involving Others 106

Appendixes   111

Appendix 1:   Resources: Learning Activities, Discussion Starters,
and Educational Approaches 111

Appendix 2:   Organizations 119

Appendix 3:   Songs 123

Appendix 4:   Experimenting with Poetry 127

Appendix 5:   Simulations and Simulation Games 129

References   133

Foreword

Many subjects taught in our schools have changed drastically since I was a student in the 1930s and 1940s. One of the delightful improvements is the Suzuki method for violin. Would that I could start again with the 5-year-olds!

Biology has now become ecology, and the various plants and animals are no longer taught as parts of a competitive predator-prey system, with inter- and intraspecies pecking orders. Now students learn about energy flows in the ecosystem, symbiotic arrangements, the food chain, and biomagnification of pollutants.

It seems that music and science have been more flexible and forward-looking than social attitudes. This was painfully apparent during the Gulf War with its exaggerated "holy cause," utterly evil enemy, and the "it's all his fault" attitude regarding the thousands of civilian deaths still occurring today.

There seem to be two kinds of orientation in the global village. The first assumes that if you are big and strong enough or have enough money, you can obtain whatever you want. The second relies on justice to promote co-operation, solidarity, and security. The first attitude breeds child abuse, battered women, rape, violent crimes, war, and nuclear bombs. It espouses "order" through force and encourages us to declare our own way to be the only "right" or "holy" or "necessary" way and then to pursue it ruthlessly. Most people no longer believe that sparing the rod makes a spoiled child or that wife beating preserves a marriage. However, there is still a lot of support for nation bashing.

In subtle ways our parent/child and teacher/child relations can teach the first attitude—"I'm bigger, do what I say." But if we teach this way, our children will grow up to do the same to younger sisters and brothers, their own children, and anyone else they are able to overpower.

This book breathes a new message. It is firmly rooted in the second attitude: Peace is not only possible, it is even desirable and fun! Don't use the ideas described here without the underlying spirit, or you will again raise a generation to kill and die. This book is important. Let your mind dream a new way and your heart warm to a new fire, and let the children teach you to be born into the twenty-first century!

Dr. Rosalie Bertell
International Institute of Concern for Public Health, Toronto
February 1992

Acknowledgments

We start by acknowledging the children with whom we have worked and played. As so often happens, we educators probably learned more than any of them. Our young friends from the WIND-Y club and our neighbors from Ste. Anne de Bellevue deserve special mention, especially Andrea and Jasmine Anderson, François Brunet, Jenny Fyon, Gordie and Jess Milligan, Brandon Runnings, Isabel and Nathan Small, and Amy Taylor. Thanks to Emmilia Assal Dowlatshahi, Jennifer Haddad, and Esther Maloney-Lebensold for their beautiful artwork. We are also grateful to the many children from the West Island YMCA day camps with whom we have worked. They introduced us to the real challenge of incorporating serious issues and deep learning into programs where the emphasis is definitely on having fun.

Our own children also deserve special acknowledgment. They cheerfully participate in regular "peace nights" and family meetings designed to keep the peace at home, and accompany us to many of the protests, ceremonies, and meetings we organize or attend. During the writing of this book, Kai and Mika helped by making suggestions, doing artwork, and offering encouragement. Three-year-old Karrie was infinitely patient while we were working, and soon figured, "If you can't beat them, join them"; she started writing her own "peace book." Finally, young Tami stayed "inside" well past her due date, giving us some bonus time for relatively uninterrupted work on the book, and has since settled into extrauterine life so smoothly that the peace here has barely been disturbed. . . .

Many adults have also contributed to this book. Some suggested ideas and useful resources, others gave enthusiastic support or read and commented on drafts, and yet others have been inspiring role models for us. Our sincere thanks, then, to Cathy Barratt, Merle Berman, Jane Blais, Patrice Brodeur, Alex Bryans, Pauline Busby, Robert Cadotte, Jacquie Dale, Sheri Dowlatshahi, Michael Dworkind, Anjula Gogia, Joan Hadrill, Ingeborg Jack, Francine Lague, Julian Lebensold, Susan Lussier, Susan Mark Landis, Suzanne Maloney-Lebensold, Serge Marsolais, Jocelyne Martin, Kathy and Jim McGinnis, Anne Noël, Andy Orkin, Mary Joan and Jerry Park, Marilyn Paxton, Marianne Perreault, and Bill Tilden.

Pat Lewis is always willing to share her experience, and kindly made available her photographs of the Kids for Peace club for inclusion here. Peggy Nickels is the finest role model we could hope for, and has always inspired us with her sincerity, hard work, meticulous attention to detail, and respectful approach to children and adults alike. She also encouraged us to get involved in international education initially, and that is where our work in this field really began.

Our thanks to Amnesty International, Greenpeace, Project Plough-shares, Earth Beat Press, and the *New Internationalist* for permission to reprint some of their statistics and graphics.

Much of our work on this book was funded by the Bursaries for Peace project, sponsored in 1987 by Harvey Giesbrecht. With the help of Sheila Segal and Rene Blouin, Harvey organized the Art Paix exhibition and auction, which featured original works donated by artists from across Canada, including Mary Pratt, Christopher Pratt, and Betty Goodwin. The bursary project was conceived and expertly implemented by Cheryl Levitt, with Mary Evans Bapst and Corinne Saunders of Health Professionals for Nuclear Responsibility (HPNR), the Quebec chapter of Canadian Physicians for the Prevention of Nuclear War (CPPNW).

CPPNW is the national affiliate of International Physicians for the Prevention of Nuclear War (IPPNW), which has a membership of over 200,000 in 61 countries and won the 1985 Nobel Peace Prize for its role in publicizing the medical aspects of the nuclear threat. Board members of CPPNW have endorsed this book. The mission statement of CPPNW reads, "Because of our concern for global health, we are committed to the prevention of war, and the promotion of nonviolent means to resolve conflict." HPNR, introducing its Bursaries for Peace project, stated, "It is the concern of health professionals to maintain and improve human health. The nuclear threat constitutes a direct threat to all life on this planet: in the event of nuclear war there can be no adequate medical response. We therefore consider it our moral obligation to prevent nuclear conflict. Furthermore, production of nuclear weapons is caus-ing disastrous environmental impacts, inducing disease and starvation in populations worldwide, and deflecting huge sums of money and technological expertise from the social sector."

While much of our educational work with children has focused on the nuclear threat and on peace, some of it has explored issues like human rights, social justice, development, international education, and ecol-ogy. One topic often flows quite naturally into another—how can we hope for peace in a world full of injustice? Or for a clean environment in a world where chemical and nuclear weapons are produced? Or for an end to the destruction of rainforests while peasants are being forced off their land by multinational companies? So, apart from resources put out by HPNR and CPPNW—which we have found invaluable—people and resources from a variety of other organizations have also helped us throughout. We especially want to acknowledge Amnesty International, Friends of the Earth, Girl Guides of Canada, Greenpeace, the Institute for Peace and Justice, Little Friends for Peace, Pacijou, the Peace-Justice-Service Commission of the Ohio Conference of the Mennonite Church, Project Ploughshares, the Social Justice Committee of Mon-treal, West Islanders for Nuclear Disarmament, and the Montreal and Ottawa YMCA International Programs.

Preface

> If we are to reach real peace in this world
> and if we are to carry on a real war against war,
> we shall have to begin with the children.
> —*Mahatma Gandhi*

WHY EDUCATE FOR SOCIAL RESPONSIBILITY?

Why should educators and parents educate children about peace, social justice, human rights, development, international issues, and ecology? When we adults were young, we were seldom burdened with such weighty and depressing issues, and we turned out okay, didn't we? Maybe. But the world has changed—is changing. There's nuclear proliferation, unprecedented environmental destruction and degradation, an ever-widening gap between rich and poor, ongoing violations of human rights, and still-emerging negative effects of television and videos on children. When we were young, it was perhaps reasonable to limit education to the three *R*s, but today all children need exposure to a fourth *R*: (social) *responsibility*.

Even in the happiest families in the world's most peaceful, just, and secure countries, children are exposed to violence, injustice, and alienation every day of their lives. They experience them in the news media; in the war games of peers; in films, videos, books, comics, and cartoons; in history and social studies lessons; in overheard adult conversations; in their own nightmares. Children need critical faculties and skills to cope with the incessant negative lessons coming at them from all directions. We must counter the slick, sick media images and prevailing cultural norms through which violence, war, oppression, discrimination, and excessive consumption are accepted uncritically or, worse, glorified. We must also challenge the complacency so prevalent among adults in privileged societies, who deny that problems like sexism, racism, injustice, or militarism exist here, in our midst. Rather than just condemning the *obvious* effects of militarism like nuclear weapons production and threats of war, we should encourage people to analyze the *hidden* social and economic consequences, particularly the effects of reduced government funding for social programs, environmental reconstruction, foreign aid, and so on.

For millions of other children, their daily experience includes fear, suffering, violence, abuse, and oppression. Some live in dysfunctional families or uncaring institutions. They need trust, acceptance, and reassurance that they are innocent victims, not wrongdoers being punished. They also need opportunities to build their self-esteem, and alternative images and perceptions of healthy, loving, and peaceful family life. Other children live in war zones or countries ravaged by gross social injustice. In these settings, peace educators must help children (and adults) to step back, analyze their situations, reflect, and rethink, before encouraging them to look ahead, reconcile, repair, and rebuild.

Consider a community-health analogy: If we raise a generation of children on a diet low in fiber and high in saturated fats, there are bound to be serious health consequences as they age. In the same way, there will be serious consequences for world peace, justice, and survival if we raise children to accept discrimination, environmental damage, and violence as a means of conflict resolution in interpersonal, family, community, national, and international disputes.

Educating for social responsibility—like all education—involves a political choice. And the *avoidance* of education for social responsibility likewise involves a political choice. With such education we can help children and youth deal with their fears, encourage them to take personal action to change situations they find unfair, and inspire them with examples of what other concerned people are doing about the same or similar problems. All of this is empowering. We could of course pretend that serious issues like environmental destruction and war don't exist. But we owe it to our children to face these issues squarely and constructively, and to help them explore the wide range of personal actions that different individuals take to tackle global problems. We believe that education for social responsibility is a fundamental part of good parenting and of early childhood, elementary, and secondary education.

Recent research has shown that students in junior and senior high schools in Canada experience severe stress living in this nuclear age. For example, 71% of the sample ranked nuclear war a "very important worry," second in frequency only to their parents' death (73%). And 61% felt they had "no personal control" in preventing nuclear war; 56% felt their parents had no control in preventing such war. At the same time, 88% said that they had not taken any action to prevent nuclear war, and 88.5% said that their parents had not taken any such action (Canadian Physicians for the Prevention of Nuclear War, 1988).

> Kids for Peace is really great;
> In our club there is no hate.
> Nobody is scared when we leave our meeting,
> For all our fears we are defeating.
> We learn lots of stuff we never knew before,
> And we are happy when we walk out the door!
> —*Alicia Barratt*

The poem reproduced above contrasts strikingly with the hopelessness, powerlessness, and despair in the CPPNW sample. It was written by nine-year-old Alicia Barratt, a member of the Kids for Peace club at Beacon Hill Elementary School in Montreal. If only more children and youth had the chance to educate themselves, organize, and take action to "defeat their fears."

There is, of course, reason to be hopeful if we can empower our children through education:

> The object of education is not to shape citizens to the uses of society, but to produce citizens able to shape a better society. (Guilbert, 1981:3.71)

Let's start now to develop globally appropriate values and attitudes in the consciences and consciousnesses of tomorrow's citizens. Let's help them learn earth-sustaining knowledge and the skills to make and keep peace. Let's plant the seeds now, so that regardless of their future personal choices (quiet reflection, spiritual work, community activism, national politics, or whatever), they live their lives in support of the earth-world and all who share it.

EDUCATIONAL PRINCIPLES GUIDING OUR PRACTICE

Our own formal training has been in adult and popular education. But we apply the same principles in our work with children, taking into account their relatively limited—but nevertheless significant—life experience. Indeed, the more we read progressive educators like Dewey (1938), Holt (1970, 1983), and Postman and Weingartner (1969), the more we realize that what we know as adult education principles are in fact also pedagogical principles.

You will discern many of our preferences and biases in this book. At the start, we want to state the principles that guide our practice as educators of both adults and children.

- Be yourself, a genuine, real human being. Don't play a stereotypical teacher's role.

- Explain to participants why you won't conform to a conventional teacher's role, and why you prefer to be a nondirective convenor, facilitator, animator, resource person, and learning partner.

- Encourage participants to be themselves in the group, behaving as full human beings also.

- Ask participants to consider trying new roles (e.g., independent learner, resource person to fellow learners, learning partner, and self- and peer-evaluator) to replace that of passive student.

- Encourage active participation rather than passive and dependent behavior.

- Respect participants, their ideas and contributions.

- Build on participants' past experiences whenever possible.

- Make it clear that you (the educator) are not an "expert" and do not have all the answers, that you view participants as learning resources for themselves, each other, and yourself.

- Take care to build and maintain a learning climate based on trust, acceptance, respect, and cooperation (see Chapter 3).

- Consult and negotiate with participants about as many administrative and content-related decisions as possible, and encourage learners to take—or at least share—responsibility for their own learning (e.g., have them choose research projects, and ask them to suggest and prioritize topics for the group to explore in future sessions, etc.).

- Recognize that interactions and relationships between participants provide powerful learning opportunities, helping them to become more aware of themselves and others in the group.

- Emphasize experiential learning, using techniques such as problem solving, simulations, drama, discussions, creative writing, and projects, rather than transmittal techniques like lectures, reading, and audiovisual presentations.

- Use humor, play, and fun to aid the learning process.

There may be other issues that you would include in the list, or some with which you disagree. Nevertheless, having a clearly articulated educational philosophy helps us to be more consistent and effective in our practice.

SOME NOTES ABOUT TERMINOLOGY

We use the term *education for social responsibility* to include peace, environmental, human rights, development, international, and social justice education. The term *global education* as used by progressive educators is an alternative that fits in most cases. When we use the terms *peace education* and *peace club* in this book, we mean *peace* in its broadest sense.

You will also notice that we don't refer to ourselves as "teachers," or to learners as "pupils" or "students"; we believe these words come with connotations of authority and subservience, control and passivity, power and powerlessness. In brainstorming ideas for the title of this book, the word *kids* kept coming up. We rejected it in favor of the more formal but perhaps more respectful word *children.* Using a new vocabulary to think and communicate about people and activities in the educational situation is a simple but potentially powerful way of avoiding an authoritarian educational role.

> Certainly, we have discovered . . . that great strides can be made if the words "teach" and "teaching" are simply subtracted from the operational lexicon. . . . Of such small language shifts, revolutions can be made. (Postman and Weingartner, 1969:47)

PEACE WORK IN THE MIDST OF WAR

We started work on this book in late 1990 and early 1991, during the build-up to and duration of the Gulf War. So even as we were thinking, talking, and writing about educating children about peace, human rights, environmental protection, and international respect, a ghastly war gripped the attention of the world. Civilians on both sides of the conflict were being maimed and killed in torture sessions and bombing raids. Oil spills and fires were polluting the seas and skies of the whole region, and the threat of massive human and ecological destruction from chemical, biological, and nuclear weapons hung over the world as thick as smog. Racist remarks, both anti-Arab and anti-Jewish, were being made openly in many quarters.

Our children—like us, and like millions of viewers and listeners around the world—spent hours transfixed as the media followed what some called the "progress" of the war with minute-by-minute coverage. Scary, video-green images of destruction mesmerized us. There were long shots of the Iraqi night sky lit up with missiles and blazing antiaircraft fire. And there was close-up footage of missiles being fired and bombs being dropped. This was almost more fun than watching violent TV cartoons. Too few of us stopped to wonder what havoc these weapons would cause when they disappeared offscreen and exploded into the homes and lives of our fellow world citizens. How impressive it all seemed to the children, and, night after night, how "normal," how "right" it became. So few people were asking the fundamental questions anymore: Is this a legitimate role for the United Nations? Why is the United States responding so strongly to *this* invasion, to *these* human rights and international law violations? What are the ultimate objectives of the superpowers in this region? Why were diplomatic and economic channels not given a fair chance? Instead, everything was reduced to a simple good-guy-versus-bad-guy equation.

Six weeks later we saw President Bush making his "victory" speech, talking of "our victorious fighting forces" and "magnificent military success." Americans seemed euphoric; bitter memories of Vietnam could at last be put to rest, they said. And with so few American casualties, no one seemed ready to consider the tens of thousands of Iraqi soldiers killed and injured; the "enemy" had been successfully depersonalized, even trivialized. Children around the world got the message: Might is right—as long as it is Western and Northern might, not Middle Eastern or Southern. And it is only Western and Northern (not Middle Eastern or Southern) lives that are worth preserving, only their deaths that are worth mourning. The age-old pattern of fear, mistrust, competition, lack of respect, and violent conflict resolution was reinforced.

No sooner was the Cold War over than the Gulf War began. And the Gulf War was no sooner over than people all around the world started thinking ugly thoughts, like "Is disarmament really a good idea?" "After all," they reasoned, "who predicted that international forces would be needed to fight in the Gulf?" And, "You can never trust *[choose one or more of the following]* Arabs, Americans, Iraqis, Europeans, Palestinians, Israelis, Canadians, Russians, Jordanians. . . ."

Should we just accept that violent conflict is inevitable, then? Must we give up on ideals like disarmament, zero nuclear weapons production, international cooperation, and equitable distribution of global wealth? Surely not. Now more than ever, we must send out alternative messages to children and their parents. Please, don't give up. Join with us and the many others swimming against the tide to educate for social responsibility.

Merryl Hammond and Rob Collins
Montreal
May 1992

Chapter 1

Raising Issues, Raising Consciousness: Learning Activities

> Techniques are tools to be used with plenty of imagination,
> and often need to be creatively adapted.
> —Arnold, Barndt, and Burke, 1985:78

    *   *   *   *   *

In the summer of 1990, Native rights were headline news in Canada. Determined to protect land they claim as traditional, Mohawks erected a roadblock at Kanesetake, near Oka, Quebec. A botched police raid on the roadblock resulted in the death of a police officer and a subsequent protracted armed standoff between Mohawk warriors and the Canadian armed forces. Mohawks in nearby Kanewake then blockaded the Mercier bridge, a major route onto the island of Montreal. A poetic gesture of solidarity.

Children got to talking about the "Oka crisis" in a peace club, and one boy said, "I think the government is being so unfair. The Mohawks have so little land left, they have to defend it. So I've made a sympathy blockade as well, in our driveway."

This put light in many eyes—ours included—and introduced a discussion about public protest and civil disobedience in the peace movement. We discuss children's participation in such protests and events later in this chapter. The memory of this child's original and eloquent action stands out. Such imagination children have. Such pragmatism. And such good hearts.

*   *   *   *   *

In this chapter (about learning activities) and the next one (about discussion starters), we are not *prescribing* techniques. There are no magical methods to create the trust and openness necessary for a learning group to tackle in positive and empowering ways such weighty issues as the nuclear threat, environmental destruction, or human rights abuses. So much depends on the learning climate and sense of community in a group that we devote the third chapter to these issues. Meanwhile, we note that

> *how* something is taught is just as important as *what* is taught. And the most important part of how something is taught is the *caring, respect,* and *shared concern* that go into it. (Werner and Bower, 1982:1.4)

In other words, our attitudes as educators are a fundamental part of the educational process. Education for social responsibility (or for any other purpose) can never be reduced to selecting techniques from some bag of methodological tricks. While there are many activities that encourage learners to explore issues more effectively, these activities in isolation can never substitute for an educator's caring, respect, and concern.

The quotation above also emphasizes that we must always consider both the *content* (what is learned) and the *process* (how learning and teaching proceed). In effective education, these two aspects dovetail and complement each other. So educators and parents concerned about human rights, justice, peace, and so on, try to make children feel safe, fairly treated, respected, and equally valued in the very educational situations in which they learn about these concepts. The learning activities we use should, whenever possible, mirror a more peaceful, just, and secure view of the earth-world and how we—and they—can live in and on it. For example, we create opportunities for all learners to participate in democratic decision making, rather than making arbitrary decisions ourselves; we openly address issues of sexism and racism when they emerge in the group; and we play cooperative rather than competitive games. And always, we try to remember that children (and adult learners too) are entitled to have *fun* while they learn, so we try to use activities that will be challenging, interesting, and enjoyable.

CHOOSING APPROPRIATE LEARNING ACTIVITIES

A peace educator says, "I want to discuss radiation and its health effects. The children must know why we are so opposed to nuclear weapons. But how can I do this in an interesting, fun, not-too-scary way?" Which of these strategies do you think would be most appropriate?

- Use a newspaper report or magazine article about victims of Chernobyl as a discussion starter.
- Start with the story *Sadako and the Thousand Paper Cranes*, based on the true story of a victim of leukemia following Hiroshima.
- Make an eye-catching poster summarizing the health effects of radiation on different parts of the body.
- Make labels indicating the health effects of radiation on different parts of the body and either stick the labels on yourself or on one of the children's bodies as you explain each.
- Brainstorm what the children already know about the subject.
- Read an extract from a medical text.
- Visit a doctor who will introduce the children to a patient undergoing radiation therapy.
- Just tell the children what the health effects of radiation are!
- Show a movie about the topic.
- Ask some children to act out the major symptoms of radiation sickness while others try to guess what they are.
- Start a discussion with an appropriate song or poem.
- Ask the children to do some research in small groups; have some go to the library, some interview health experts, and so on.

Whatever you answered is potentially the best answer. So many factors must be considered, for example, the ages of the children in the group, the specific objectives of the session, time allocation, availability of transport, and so on. There is no substitute for a thorough situation analysis (see Chapter 4). So this introductory exercise reminds us that there is seldom one approach, strategy, or activity that is better than all others. We can only offer ideas to stimulate your imagination.

A few introductory points should be made. First, original, homemade activities usually work best. So innovate, take a chance—only you know the precise circumstances and objectives of your work. Second, *variety* piques interest and holds attention, so don't overuse particular learning activities just because you feel most comfortable with them. (On the other hand, don't use a technique that feels gimmicky or makes you feel unconfident. The children will sense your lack of conviction and the session may fail miserably.) Third, any learning is more effective if it builds on the *past experience* of the learner, so plan to incorporate the knowledge, experience, and interests of group members. Lastly,

> generally speaking, one technique is usually not sufficient to investigate a theme. Usually it needs to be combined with others to allow a group to deepen its understanding of the areas under consideration. (Arnold, Barndt, and Burke, 1985:78)

With these general points made, we'll now describe some learning activities we and other educators have found useful in our work with children. (The whole subcategory of learning activities that can be used as discussion starters is dealt with in the next chapter.)

READING

Children thoroughly enjoy reading about nonviolent, peace-promoting, earth-saving heroes. Try true stories about inspiring people—both women and men, of course—like Harriet Tubman, Martin Luther King, Nelson Mandela, Mahatma Gandhi, and Florence Nightingale. Or a fictional story like *The Paper Bag Princess* by Robert Munsch, which challenges some of our deepest-rooted sexist assumptions.

We don't censor traditional fairy tales and other stories as being too sexist or racist. Rather, we read them and then critically discuss the author's assumptions about whoever is stereotyped in the story. When a sexist author constantly refers to animals or other characters by male pronouns, simply change "he" to "she" and "his" to "hers." If necessary, change the ending to promote justice: let the rescuing hero be a woman in the retelling; turn the swift steed into a wheelchair; make the fair, blond maiden into a black-eyed, olive-skinned one instead. We were delighted when our three-year-old daughter insisted on "all the King's horses and all the King's *women*" and "one for the little *girl* who lives down the lane" when singing nursery rhymes—with no (conscious) prompting or coaching from us, either!

You may also want to help children become more critical about the kinds of books that make it onto the bestseller lists in our society. In how many are the main characters either dominating or violent? How many are swindlers or murderers, as opposed to caring people? Why?

And then there are the many books that glorify war. We once received a promotional flyer from Time-Life Books inviting us to "team up for battle in *The Armored Fist.* . . . Join in on some of the fiercest land wars in modern military history, from behind the controls of the world's most fearsome armored assault vehicles."

All the King's women: a nonsexist retelling of Humpty Dumpty.

Our 13-year-old son looked puzzled. "But they are trying to make out that war is exciting." Precisely. The flyer does not refer to the human costs of war. There is no mention of casualties, no civilian victims, no overcrowded hospitals with inadequate medical supplies, no ongoing suffering of communities whose means of subsistence and survival have been destroyed. Nor will the environmental costs of these wars be analyzed. And nor will the book they are promoting with such pride educate us about the social services that could have been paid for with the billions of dollars spent on these ghastly war machines, or about nonviolent alternatives to using an "armored fist" every time there is a potential conflict. When will the publishers of such books realize that war is not some new computer game to be marketed for its "dramatic" qualities? How can we let publishers know that such books make us sick?

Appendix 1 lists some of the books and other resources we have found most useful in our work.

COMPOSING AND WRITING

Given time, inspiration, and encouragement, most children enjoy writing poems, stories, essays, songs, prayers, graffiti, "wise sayings," and slogans. Many also like to compose pieces for the piano, recorder, guitar, or other musical instruments.

We try to stimulate writing and composing as a follow-up to discussions, movies, and other learning activities. Later, some of it can be further used. For example, graffiti can be combined in a mural or collage, and copies of letters to government leaders can be used in a subsequent role-play or simulation game where children pretend to be the President or Prime Minister, reading their letters (and others supporting the opposite view) before deciding on a policy. Appendix 4 includes examples of poems written by children at Beacon Hill Elementary School, and brief guidelines compiled by Pat Lewis for educators teaching poetry.

This poem by Tara MacDonald, one of Pat's pupils, was written when she was 10 years old.

My Wish ☆

If I had a wish, I'd wish that everyone,
everywhere,
Would learn to live in peace, and to love and
to care,
For every single person, no matter what colour
their skin,
On what religion they have, or what country
they live in.
Loving and caring for everyone - that has got to
be the key
To making this world a better place to be.

Tara MacDonald

Letter writing to politicians, newspaper editors, and children's magazines is also popular. Members of the Kids for Peace club in Beaconsfield even wrote letters to Santa, asking him not to give war toys as gifts!

If the children are very young, we ask them to compose mentally or dictate to us, and we take notes using their own words and phrases. We then read our notes back to them to check whether they want to add or delete anything. The brief letter below and the much longer one about the Gulf War (see pages 77–78) were both drafted in this way by 5- to 11-year-old members of a peace club.

```
The Rt. Hon. Prime Minister
House of Commons
Ottawa, Ontario
Canada K1A 1A0
                                          10 August, 1990
Dear Mr. Mulroney,

                  re: THE ENVIRONMENT

    Meech Lake and other problems like that seem to be
keeping you too busy to think about the environment. We are
cutting down too many trees; we are wasting paper instead
of recycling it; too many factories are polluting the air,
the ground and the water; there is a big hole in the ozone
layer caused by CFCs; we are creating too much garbage
because of overpackaging.
    We need new laws and law enforcement to solve these
problems. Please fit in some time to think about all this.
And please respond to us as soon as possible.

Yours truly,
```

Jasmine Anderson (8)

Jessie McIlligan (age 8)

BRANDON BURNING (a=6)

ANDREA ANDERSON (5)

GORDON MCILIGAN (6)

With several groups of children, we have enjoyed using a technique we call cooperative poetry writing. We start by brainstorming ideas related to the theme. For example, "What first comes to mind when we say the word *war*?" Then we reorder and edit the items to make a poem. Sometimes we also illustrate the poem for visual impact (see page 87, for example). The poems about war and peace included here were cooperatively written by young members of the West Islanders for Nuclear Disarmament-Youth (WIND-Y) club. Other suitable topics include nature and pollution, justice and injustice, and violence and nonviolence.

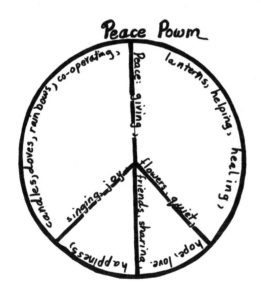

We have used the war-and-peace poetry exercise in several groups. Each time we find that the lengths of the two brainstormed lists are very different. The "war" lists are generated so fast it is often difficult for us to get all the ideas down on paper. The acuity of the ideas is also excellent: children can name war machines and weapons we have not yet even heard of! But when we ask them to think about peace, there is a long silence. Someone, trying hard, will say something like, "my bedroom." And someone else, relieved to have something to work with at last, goes off on a tangent about her duvet, or his cupboard; and only after a while do they realize that we have strayed far from the original idea of peace. We then prompt them with questions like, "How does peace sound? Smell? Look? Taste? Feel to the touch? How does it make you feel inside?"

At the end of the brainstorm, we ask the children to look at their lists and to comment on what they see. It does not take them long to say something like, "Gee, we know a lot more about war than about peace!" We then ask them to consider some of the major influences on their lives: TV, comics, movies, toys, sticker books, and so on. They start to become more aware of the literal "bombardment" of war-related information and hype to which they are subjected and, if they're honest, to which they willingly subject themselves. Some children have been so motivated by this exercise that they want to change their TV-viewing and buying habits.

Another idea for a cooperative writing project is to ask the group to generate ideas for a policy statement, press release, or charter. This stimulates children to analyze critically their situations and is a good team-building exercise. The Youth Declaration included below was drafted by a group of about two hundred Soviet and American youth in Moscow in 1988.

The Youth Declaration for the Future

We, the children of today and the future adults of the twenty-first century, desire to make a positive difference in our world and secure the survival of all life on the planet. We request that governments, in their role as representatives of the people, establish political and social priorities to enhance the welfare of all kingdoms of life. As Youth Ambassadors of the Soviet Union and the United States, we worked together in Moscow for the world's first youth summit. For four days we met to discuss how we envision our future and how we can work together to create a better world for today and tomorrow. Seven committees of students from 10 to 18 years of age declare that:

1. The youth of the world desire more avenues for communication with one another.

2. Educational systems must prepare everyone for the twenty-first century by creating a strong foundation for peace.

3. Opportunities should be provided that enable youth to develop their full potential so that substance abuse will be eliminated.

4. Individuals must take responsibility for caring for the earth that supports us.

5. Increase the love within families and communities.

6. Cultural exchanges be established to increase international trust and understanding.

7. Replace global competition with global cooperation.

This declaration is submitted by the youth of the world to every government on earth, requesting adult support in carrying out our visions for the future. We acknowl-

edge our relationship to our planet and each other and
we want all people to work together to improve the
world we share, today and tomorrow.

(Holistic Education Review, vol. 1, no. 4, 1988:51)

Valuable lessons are learned in an exercise like this. Participants
have to collaborate, respect each others' ideas, lobby, reach consensus,
and be creative with language. They are empowered by the process of
trying to capture in words such important, complex, and lofty ideals.
The dialogue and analysis that precedes the drafting of the charter
challenges people and raises new questions. Commitment to the group
and to the ideas being expressed also develops. The finished product—
the declaration—is concrete evidence of their cooperative work, giving
them a sense of personal and collective achievement.

You can also ask children to make up new sayings to replace ones that
use military or antienvironmental notions such as "they won the battle
but lost the war," "kill two birds with one stone," and others. And you
can have them play with words, for example by challenging children who
know about the three *R*s of environmentalism—*reduce, re-use* and
recycle—to think of a fourth *R*. Ideas include *rethink* our attitudes,
reorder our priorities, *reclaim* our heritage, and *resolve* to do something
practical to save the earth.

ART AND CRAFTWORK

In the informal and relaxed atmosphere around a large table,
surrounded by papers, paints, glue, dye, or clay, a different dynamic
often develops. We often end a long session with activities like these,
playing some appropriate music in the background. When some people
have completed the activity and while others are finishing, it's generally
a good time to refer back to a previous discussion or to introduce an idea
for the next session. One of the children often raises an issue for
discussion at this point, too.

Sometimes we ask children to work on *individual* art or craft projects.
This is easy—it requires no cooperation beyond the need to share the
available materials. Usually, we plan for them to take their pictures or
paintings home as mementos for themselves and as a way of giving their
parents and siblings some idea of what the group is doing. (See Chapter
5 for more on involving family members.) If we keep their work to
display, we make sure that everyone's contribution gets equal attention;
we don't try to judge which is "best."

At other times, we ask the group to work *cooperatively* on a project,
such as making posters, collages, murals, or printing fabric. To
complete the project, children need to work collaboratively and democratically in planning the work, allocating tasks, and getting it done. We

discover once again that restraint and cooperation are often in short supply. We are so unaccustomed to collaborating; it is much easier to *talk* about cooperation than to do it. We all need to practice this skill much more.

One way to compromise is to ask each child to work on a section of a larger project that will be assembled at the end. Children can use paint, markers, or sewing to decorate small pieces of fabric, which later get sewn into a large flag or quilt. Or they can color small cut-outs of plants and animals to be pasted onto cardboard to make a large forest. Or the children can make the flags of various countries to hang in a "Friends of the World" banner. In this way, young children can be spared the frustration of having to cooperate all through the project, yet benefit from the sense of group accomplishment when their individual contributions become part of a larger and more impressive product.

Peace quilt by Kids for Peace.

COOPERATIVE GAMES

When you stop to analyze most children's games, they tend either to be competitive or to place one person, like the "it" in tag or the "seeker" in hide-and-seek, in a stressful position. Since we are dealing with issues of peace, cooperation and harmony, we like the games we play to mirror some of these principles. Instead of playing win-lose games that leave some people feeling beaten or like losers, we try to play win-win games in which all children can have fun, do their best, and help others.

The *Co-op Games Manual* by Jim Deacove (1974, 1980) helped us make the initial leap from conventional to cooperative games. He has also compiled *Co-op Marble Games* (1987a), *Co-op Parlour Games* (1987b), and *Co-op Sports Manual* (1982) for use with adults and older children. The resources by Orlick (1978) and Sobel (1982) are also excellent. Through Family Pastimes (see Appendix 2 for address), Jim also produces and markets an excellent selection of co-op board games, puzzles, and so on. This statement is from the introduction to their sales catalogue:

> The initial impulse to play a game is social; that is, we bring out a game because we want to do something together. How ironic then that in most games, we spend all our efforts trying to bankrupt someone, destroy their armies, in other words, to get rid of one another! We soon learn how to pick on the other person's weaknesses in order to eliminate him or her from the game. People of different ages and abilities should be able to play side by side, each making their best contribution. In a cooperative game, someone young and little can play with others older and bigger and not worry about being wiped out. We are all there at the end of it. A simple, common party game for socializing youngsters illustrates our point. Musical Chairs fosters aggression and elimination. Played cooperatively (see our *Co-op Games Manual*), you'll witness how hugging replaces pushing, how ability and strength are used to help rather than push out of the way. . . . In sum, games are used in various settings and for various reasons. Socialization, entertainment, academic learning, character growth, etc. Whatever your objectives, we invite you to realize them by cooperative means.

When we analyze and discuss games with them, children not only understand the reasons for playing cooperatively, but they really enjoy the chance to play this way. Soon they think up cooperative adaptations of traditional games for themselves.

We adapted Deacove's (1974:13–14) game of Lost and Found to make up a game we call Red Cross Rescue, a cooperative variation of hide-and-seek. We use another variation of hide-and-seek, Free the Detainees, for sessions on human rights in which we discuss "disappearances" and detention without trial. Another fun game is Peacemaker, an adaptation of tag made up by François Brunet, an 11-year-old member of WIND-Y. Brief descriptions of all these games follow. Feel free to adapt the rules to suit your own purposes and topics, or encourage children to make up new games themselves.

Red Cross Rescue

Imagine that there is a terrible war raging, guns shooting, bombs dropping. We have been wounded and have to find a safe place to hide, waiting for the Red Cross ambulance (the "seeker," who counts while we all hide) to come and rescue us. As soon as the "ambulance" finds us and we get treated, we recover and run with the ambulance to rescue the next casualty. The last person to be rescued is the ambulance in the next round. (This game still draws its inspiration from war. You could substitute mountaineers needing rescue after a snowstorm, canoeists washed away in a flood, or victims of a hurricane or volcano eruption.)

Free the Detainees

One person, the "liberator," counts while all the rest—the "detainees"—hide. The liberator searches and when s/he finds a detainee, the two of them go off in search of other detainees to liberate.

Peacemaker

One person is the Peacemaker. Everyone else runs around pretending to be soldiers with guns, trying to shoot each other. The Peacemaker chases the soldiers, and as soon as s/he touches one, the imaginary gun turns into a flower or other peace symbol and the soldier becomes a Peacemaker too. Now there are two Peacemakers to stop the war! The game continues until all soldiers have been converted into Peacemakers. Then a new Peacemaker, perhaps the last soldier to be transformed, begins the game again.

For international education, we play games and use toys from other countries and cultures. Children enjoy the novelty of this and learn to appreciate different cultures.

> As we try to help children become members of the global community, it is important to introduce games that foster an appreciation of other cultures and encourage attitudes of cooperation and sharing. Games from developing countries are a fine way to help children begin to understand that these countries have something of value to offer them. A major feature of games from developing countries is that they are accessible to all: they cost almost nothing—usually a handful of pebbles or a few sticks are required—and they can be played everywhere. (Montreal YMCA International Programs, 1985a:44)

USING OUR BODIES

Children need to be active and physical a lot of the time. Think of ways to build dances (perhaps folk dances from other cultures), bending and stretching exercises, and other forms of movement into a session. In one group, someone suggested making "human peace signs," and the children all had fun experimenting with different ways of draping themselves on the floor to achieve a good result.

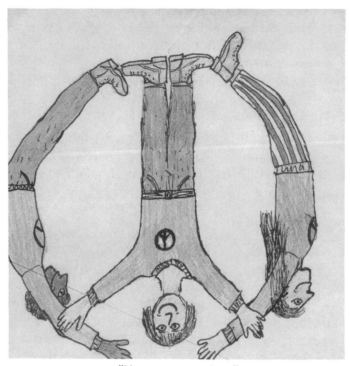

"Human peace sign."

During an environmental session, we asked children to "become" pollutants, moving around the room as a pollutant would. It was wonderful—though depressing—to see oil slicks slithering over the floor, smog particles twirling around on tip-toe with their arms in the air, exhaust fumes hunched over making great billowing movements with their arms, and so on. Sound effects can work well too. Try miming to well-known songs, like "I'm a little green frog, sitting in the water." Or play charades, asking each child to choose a favorite animal to mime while the others guess what it is.

An activity we call the Human Map can also work well during international education sessions. We make cards with the names of various countries, including a fair representation of Third World countries, and ask each child to "be" one country. They arrange themselves close to neighboring countries, leaving empty spaces to represent the oceans. With older children, you can explain the objective, give each person a card, and ask them to refer to a world map or globe in order to create a reasonably accurate human map. Younger children will need lots of help to get into position and stay there long enough for everyone to be placed before the map collapses. We end this exercise by asking the "countries" to stretch out to others that, though far away geographically (and often culturally and ideologically, too), are part of the world family of nations. Gradually, the divisions between countries and continents are narrowed, and the whole world joins in a large circle, with everyone linking hands in unity. A song like "To everyone in all the world I reach my hand, I shake their hand" can then be sung and mimed.

Serge Marsolais (1990:30) asked children to try carrying buckets of water on their heads like children in many parts of the Third World have to do every day. This is another example of how innovative educators can use physical activities that simultaneously burn up energy and help children learn.

Another fun technique, used by popular educators who work with adults but which we have found equally appropriate with children, is called sculpturing.

> Sculpturing is an exercise that uses people (rather than clay)
> to create a visual image of a particular theme. (Farlow,
> 1986:9)

With adults, sculpturing is used to represent complex relationships between various elements in a situation. For example, in one workshop Arnold and Burke (1983:30) asked participants to make a sculpture showing how the North American media was portraying the war in Nicaragua. Someone stood on a chair (to show power), representing the Soviet Union, while someone else stood near this person on the floor, representing Cuba. A person representing the United States also stood on a chair on the far side of the room (to show ideological distance from Cuba and the Soviet Union).

We have used complex sculpturing like this even with young children. When Iraq invaded Kuwait in August 1990, we had a detailed discussion with 5- to 11-year-old WIND-Y peace club members about whether they thought that Canada and other nations should send troops to the Gulf. After studying a world map, discussing the cultural and religious differences between the opposing forces, and considering the implications of war, we wanted to summarize at the end of the session and spontaneously tried a human sculpture. After a brief explanation, the children responded eagerly. "I'll be the oil," said one, getting down on her knees and waving her arms overhead to make spurting movements. "I'm big, powerful Iraq," said another, jumping onto a chair and flexing his biceps. And so the sculpture grew: the Iraqi army pointing imaginary guns, chemical, biological, and perhaps even nuclear weapons at the Saudis and Israelis; crushed Kuwait, kneeling under Iraq's chair; the United States and other Western nations linking hands with Egypt and Saudi Arabia; someone kneeling and praying to Allah to represent Moslem fundamentalism; someone else bending in prayer before a wall to represent Zionists at the wailing wall. Afterward, one of the children suggested that they write a letter to the prime minister of Canada and the president of the U.S.A. to tell them that war was an awful choice. Everyone agreed, and a long letter (reproduced in Chapter 4) was written down as the children brainstormed and contributed phrases and ideas.

Human sculpture of the situation before the Gulf War: child artist's impression.

Kids for Peace rap and act out movements in "peace-full exercises." In this photo, they are rapping, "Run and run, break a gun." Others are "Fly like a dove for peace and love," "Bend and bend, shake with a friend," "Hop, hop, hop, make wars stop," and "All wars can cease with a circle of peace."

Kids for Peace rap, "Run and run, break a gun!"

For Earth Day, we adapted this idea and asked participants to join us in some "earthy exercises": "Stretch and bend, make pollution end," "Sit then stand, let's get whaling banned," and "Touch the turf, we'll save the Earth."

DRAMATIC WORK

Two commonly used dramatic techniques, role-plays and skits, are described with other discussion starters in Chapter 2. You can also consider mime, puppetry (see Condon and McGinnis, 1988), plays, face painting, masks, cooperative story telling (see Montreal YMCA International Programs, 1985a:63), and dressing up.

One fun way to help children address their prejudices is to ask them to come dressed up as a child from another country or culture. Each person then parades before the others, who guess where s/he is from. Once they have identified the country, located it on the world map, and perhaps said something about the

Dressed up as Tsonga mother and child.

major languages and religions of the region, you can "rename" the child with a common name from that country. When the whole group has been introduced and named, the discussion can focus on the similarities and differences between children in your country and children from the countries represented in the circle.

They may initially focus on *differences* like clothing, language, beliefs, skin color, facial features, and customs, feeling themselves to be quite separate from children elsewhere. In a spontaneous role-play technique, we addressed each child by her or his new (foreign) name: "Stephan, how do you feel when your parents don't understand you?"; "Thandi, do your knees bleed when you fall and scrape them?"; "Abdul, when your puppy died, how did you feel?"; "Maria, how do you feel the day before your birthday party?"; "Zinzi, what do you do when someone tickles you all over?"; and so on. This really helped them "get under the skin" of their imaginary counterparts. Some of them were visibly excited to discover that children who looked and dressed and *seemed* so different were also very similar. "They" also laugh, cry, and bleed; we must all be human after all! We then reinforce this sense of unity with children all over the world with an appropriate song, story, or poem.

With older children, we tackle the issue of cultural and racial stereotyping head on. We ask what derogatory names they have heard used to refer to people from Pakistan, Africa, Japan, Germany, or elsewhere. What prejudices do some people have against Jews, Muslims, immigrants, the elderly, the handicapped, the homeless, women, or others? Is it fair to classify everyone in a particular cultural, national, or social group in that way? Have they ever been victimized by a stereotype? How does/would it feel? What effect does stereotyping have on our relationships, on community life, on world peace? What racist (or sexist, etc.) thoughts or behaviors do they have? What can we do to break down stereotypes? (See Condon and McGinnis, 1988:58–59, for a barrier-breaking exercise, Try on My Shoe.)

MUSIC

Beat, jingle, hum, sing, play, strum: children love music. We use recordings by popular children's artists; play music from other countries and cultures; change the mood with upbeat modern or evocative classical music; lead the group in a song they can follow; or sing more complicated songs ourselves. Appendix 1 lists some songs we like, and the words and music for some of our original songs are in Appendix 3.

Members of the WIND-Y group singing.

Why not include children in music making (rather than passive listening)? Delight them by asking them to play on instruments from other cultures, on simple homemade instruments like dry beans in a coffee can, or on easy-to-play instruments like xylophones, triangles, harmonicas, recorders, tambourines, and drums. And encourage them to write their own songs, perhaps using the tune of a well-known nursery song, Christmas carol, or pop song. Songs about the various topics being studied work well, and children may enjoy cooperating to write a theme song for their club. Arnold and Burke (who write in the context of popular education with Canadian adults, but whose point is equally valid for most Western children) recommend that animators help groups to "create culture" instead of uncritically "consuming" it.

> In our society, where we are largely consumers of culture,
> the act of putting together a short play or writing a song can
> in itself be empowering for people. (Arnold and Burke,
> 1983:29)

FOOD, COOKING, AND EATING

Did you ever consider using a banana or a tuna tin as a discussion starter or visual aid? Help children appreciate other cultures by exposing them to new foods and eating utensils. (Condon and McGinnis, 1988:54–55, have an exercise emphasizing that no eating custom is superior to any other.) For international education sessions, we bring exotic fruits and vegetables for children to examine and taste, asking, "What color do you think this fruit is inside? Do you think it has seeds? What size and shape?" An "international fruit salad," using unusual ingredients from other countries, also works well. These food-related activities combine well with dressing up, playing music, and reading stories from the country concerned.

Depending on the objectives of the session, food and fruit can be used as a discussion starter about topics like exploitation (consider fruits like bananas grown in Third World countries where peasants are forced off their land, employed as wage laborers by multinational companies, exposed to poor working conditions and toxic pesticides, and paid inadequate wages), injustice (see Appendix 5, "Some feast while others starve"), and environmental destruction (e.g., beef production for export causes destruction of rain forests, whaling to meet the demand of Eastern restaurants continues to endanger the species, drift-net fishing for tuna needlessly kills dolphins and other marine life).

If facilities permit, simple cooking and baking projects can be lots of fun (see Montreal YMCA International Program, 1985a:51–54). For example, "peace cookies" could be baked, iced with peace signs, hearts, or other symbols, and shared among families or brought to a peace celebration.

SIMULATIONS AND SIMULATION GAMES

Some simulations involve simple demonstrations (see Chapter 4, where we describe a simple glass bowl, water, and coloring demonstration to illustrate how pollution spreads, for example). Others may be more elaborate and expensive. The Ottawa YM-YWCA Children's International Center, for example, builds mini-villages to simulate life in other countries.

Young children enjoy going on imaginary trips by car, boat, train, or air. When we get to the desired destination, we show slides, photographs, or artifacts from the area, and sometimes ask the children to interview us as we pretend to be a typical farm worker or villager from the country. We find that a large colored photograph of children from the country (e.g., from a New Internationalist or Amnesty International calendar) is especially powerful. We "introduce" the children in the photo using common names from that country, and use them as reference points in subsequent discussions, asking questions like, "Why do you suppose Pedro has no shoes?" and "What do you think Maria ate for breakfast today?"

Serge Marsolais (1990:25–28) describes a realistic boat trip to Nicaragua that he simulated with YMCA day campers. Four people made waves with a large sheet of blue fabric, while someone held up a mast and others held strips of fabric for sails; everyone else was in the ship made of fabric. A tape with the sound of waves played in the background, and Serge showed where the ship was moving on a world map. The children all swayed their bodies to simulate the rolling movement of the ship, and occasional sightings of dolphins, whales, and islands were included in the imaginary voyage. On their return to Canada, Serge pretended to be a person who had stayed behind during the trip, and got them to review and summarize their learning about Nicaragua by asking them what they had seen and heard during their visit. We have since adapted these ideas with several groups of children, including preschoolers, to educate them about conditions in other countries and specifically to motivate them (and encourage their parents) to support the annual Tools for Peace campaign. They really enjoy the simulations, and at subsequent sessions many of them ask if they can go to visit their imaginary foreign friends again.

Simulation games can be quite complex and may need detailed preparation beforehand. But they can be extremely powerful learning activities, well worth the time and effort they take. Appendix 5 includes some simple simulation games and statistics for peace and human rights education. Adapt these ideas to suit your needs, or better still, design your own simulation games. We found the books by Hope and Timmel (1984) very useful for stimulating our thinking about simulations.

Preschoolers on an imaginary boat trip:
laundry baskets are boats, blue sheets are the ocean.

RESEARCH PROJECTS

To encourage children to take greater control over and responsibility for their own learning, you might ask them to do some research and to bring their findings to the group as a whole. Alternatively, pairs or small groups could get some practice at cooperating while working together on a project. Their motivation will be higher if they have suggested or chosen the topic themselves.

Younger children will need help thinking of methods to find the required information for a project. There are many possibilities: a telephone interview with a government official, journalist, local peace activist, or human rights advocate, for example; a visit to the local library or museum; a discussion with a teacher; interviews with adults or children who have themselves experienced war or who have fled as refugees from war zones or countries where human rights violations are common, and so on.

Reporting back to the group can be done in writing or orally. Either way, you could work with individuals or groups to prepare a clear and polished presentation with suitable visual aids. Older children may enjoy including their findings in a letter to a newspaper editor or politician. Some may be stimulated to write an essay, short story, or poem, which could be submitted to a children's magazine (see Appendix 1 for ideas) or for a competition at school. This is a good time to invite parents and siblings to hear what work the children have been doing.

VISITS AND VISITORS

Sometimes a visit (to a museum, arboretum, university, hospital, park, or memorial) provides just the excitement and novelty a group needs. Preparation beforehand should include a session in which children phrase questions they want answered or pose problems they want solved. This ensures that they will be more actively engaged in the visit, rather than just passive observers.

Given time and financial constraints and transport problems, it is often necessary to compromise by bringing visitors to the group rather than taking the group on a visit. Invite a wildlife expert, curator of a museum, person from another country, or child member of another local peace club to visit. Once again, preparation before the visitor comes is essential if the group is to get their needs met. They could brainstorm a list of issues or questions they'd like the visitor to deal with, or set up a debate in which one of them opposes the view the visitor will take, and so on. We do this well in advance, so that we can communicate with the visitor beforehand.

TAKING ACTION

When children feel strongly about an issue, we believe they should take action in the same kinds of ways we do. For example, they may want to write letters to politicians, participate in protests against the sale of war toys outside toy stores at Christmas time, attend candlelight vigils and marches for peace, or join a sit-in outside government offices to protest environmentally unsound policies. This gives them a sense that they are participants in real events, *makers* of history—to whatever small extent we all can be—rather than powerless observers of it. Also, participating in such events helps children feel connected to others who are concerned, thus overcoming the sense of helplessness and isolation that paralyzes so many people. If a protest they have participated in receives media coverage, they will be excited to watch the news on TV or to keep a newspaper clipping, and this kind of reinforcement—that ordinary people can and sometimes do make a difference—may stimulate future involvement and activism.

The anniversary of the bomb dropped on Hiroshima (August 6) is one we have commemorated with children, who thoroughly enjoy planning and participating in an annual community Peace Ceremony (see Chapter 4 for details). The planning process is empowering for children, and it is an excellent time to review a lot of the work we have done with a group during the preceding weeks and months. The ceremony itself gives the children a chance to display talents like singing, acting, or arts and crafts; to educate a broader audience of parents, siblings, and neighbors; and, with media coverage, to reach an even wider audience. Candlelit lanterns floating on water (in our case, a neighbor's swimming pool) at night bring a very moving, spiritual element to the final part of the ceremony. It is not always easy to create a sense of real awe or wonder in children as they get older, much less with hardened suburban adults. But even reluctantly participating parents have been touched by these child-led ceremonies.

WIND-Y members, friends, and families at a neighborhood peace ceremony.

There are many other commemorative ceremonies and internationally observed occasions in which children can participate. The Kids for Peace club, for example, recently marked Earth Day, World Hunger Day, International Peace Day, Remembrance Day, and International Women's Day. For international education, you may want to organize ceremonies to recognize people from other countries, cultures, or religions who are celebrating a festival or commemorating a historical event.

Other types of action children may want to take include signing letters and petitions, participating in consumer boycotts, donating part of their pocket money and earnings to organizations working for peace and justice, participating in exchange programs, forming direct links with children in other countries or communities, and so on.

Friends of ours in South Africa, Dale and Tish White, told us about a community program during the height of the township violence, when extremists from opposing political factions were burning each other's homes. Community workshops and other peace-building interventions were organized, and the same youngsters who had burned each other's homes then worked together to rebuild and repair the damaged homes. Such meaningful action. Such powerful, concrete expressions of reconciliation.

Chapter 2
Discussion Starters

A good discussion is like a fire, which provides light, warmth, and fellowship for all those present. Gradually, every log starts to burn and contributes to the brightness and heat.
— *Hope and Timmel, 1984:57*

*   *   *   *   *

The children had all planned and practiced a role-play about discrimination, and were waiting for the small group that had drawn the first straw to come "on stage." Then they watched—half-smiling at the excellent acting, half-frowning at the ugliness of the scene portrayed. A girl with one arm tucked into her shirt and the other held stiffly at an awkward angle limped slowly, painfully over the grass. A group of noisy, bouncing children came toward her. When they saw her, they stopped, pointed, sniggered, and laughed out loud. Then they imitated her limp and ran off, laughing cruelly. The role-play ended with the handicapped girl slumped over, shaking her head sadly, looking at the ground.

The audience applauded, the actors grinned, and the "star" took a bow. Several of us wiped away our tears. We congratulated the actors and then asked everyone to sit closer together to discuss the role-play.

*   *   *   *   *

It's a real challenge to balance the need for discussion about serious issues like war, global environmental problems, human rights violations, economic exploitation, and racial prejudice with children's relatively short attention spans and their need for learning activities that are often physical. Don't neglect discussion or dismiss it as something that only teens and adults can handle. But do make discussions more active and interesting by using techniques like an attention-getting discussion starter, initial small-group work, brainstorming sessions, or asking children to make notes of their own ideas first.

A lively discussion is much more likely to follow an appropriate discussion starter than simply stating the topic and asking participants what they think. We particularly like discussion starters that engage participants emotionally as well as intellectually. Some discussion starters may even double as ice breakers (see Chapter 3). But don't forget that the purpose of a discussion starter is literally to *start* a discussion, so allow enough time for the discussion itself. Let's consider some discussion starters that work well with children.

ROLE-PLAYS

Role-plays like the one described at the start of this chapter are short sketches (usually 1–5 minutes) in which a specific point is illustrated. They often have a powerful emotional impact on the actors and audience. Actors may be members of the learning group or adults, and the "script" can be made up by the animator or by learners themselves. Acting is fun and role-plays—being so brief—can include even young children.

Children 8 years and older can cope well with and thoroughly enjoy participating in and making up role-plays. Younger children often do best with a prepared script, or just watching and discussing a role-play performed by others. We find that children like the sense of completion they get from acting out opposite scenarios, such as before/after situations (e.g., behaving in an environmentally destructive way before becoming informed, and then behaving in an earth-friendly way afterward) or negative/positive ones (e.g., violent versus nonviolent conflict resolution in a family).

The first time a group is exposed to role-plays, we provide the script, play roles ourselves, and prepare volunteers for their roles. We ask the audience to work on something else while the actors discuss the role-play and practice briefly in another room. Later on, once children are familiar with the technique, they make up their own scripts and allocate roles themselves; we just provide the topic or theme to be role-played.

After a role-play, we lead the discussion by asking:

- **What did you see happening in the role-play?** This summary is necessary before any discussion to ensure that everyone in the group grasped the major point of the play. Otherwise, the discussion itself will be confused.

- **Does this kind of thing happen in real life?** Here, we want to give people a chance to accept or deny the validity of the point being made. If they feel that the role-play was too exaggerated, they will not take it or the discussion seriously. Also, we want to help the group generalize from the specific situation portrayed (e.g., prejudice against handicapped people) to similar situations (e.g., racial, sexual, or religious prejudice). Generalizing is difficult for many children, so allow enough time.

- **Why does this kind of thing happen?** Help the children dig deeper to understand the causes of a problem. Otherwise, they may simply judge the "bad guys" and exclude themselves self-righteously— "I'd never do such a thing; I'm not part of the problem."

- **How do you feel about this problem?** Give children a chance to reflect on and share their feelings. Role-plays are often quite emotional, so participants and observers may need to let off some emotional steam.

- **Finally, what can we do to change and improve the situation?** This is the climax of the session, so don't run out of time before children can tackle this question. They are usually so involved and motivated that they generate innovative solutions to which they feel committed.

SKITS

Skits are short discussion starters that often use a combination of drama and simple props like handmade puppets, stuffed animals or toys, flags, scarves, and hats to illustrate a point or act as a metaphor for real life. The children may either be involved in the action "on stage" or as members of the audience. After the skit, we ask questions to stimulate thinking and discussion: "What did you see happening in this skit? What might this represent in real life? How did you feel . . . ? Does this ever happen in real life? What could we do . . . ?" We strongly recommend the resource by Condon and McGinnis (1988) for ideas about skits.

TESTIMONIALS

Try inviting a guest to talk about their personal experiences and answer questions. For example, in a peace education session, the testimonial of a refugee from a war-torn country could be very moving. Or in sessions about human rights and avoiding prejudice, include testimonials from members of minority groups like immigrants, handicapped children, or Native Americans. Sensitively handled, and with preparation of the group ahead of time, these can be powerful learning experiences that stimulate lively and action-oriented discussions.

GRAPHICS

There's no doubt: a relevant picture is worth a thousand words. Visual images can arouse emotions and responses that other discussion starters fail to arouse. A dry, theoretical discussion about deforestation, for example, can be transformed by showing a series of photographs of a forest before, during, and after clear cutting. Participants become more emotionally committed to the topic—and often to taking action—once they have visually identified with it. This was particularly striking in some work we did with preschoolers recently. We were educating them about conditions in Nicaragua for the Tools for Peace campaign, and one of the visual aids we used

Amnesty International poster,
"Child of the Disappeared."
*"My four brothers and I are looking for our father.
They took him away and nobody knows why, or where."*

was a large calendar picture of two Central American children, who we named Maria and Lucas. A week later at our next session, several of the children asked about Maria and Lucas by name and referred back to details they had noted in the picture, such as their worn clothing and bare feet. We were struck by the powerful impact a simple aid like that could have.

Likewise, a teenager may know all about human rights violations in Central America, quoting statistics, telling the group which countries are the worst offenders, and so on. But her heart may not be in it, and she may never be moved to action by all this information and theoretical knowledge. However, when she sees a sensitive poster like "Child of the Disappeared," produced by Amnesty International, she may be so emotionally affected that she turns the discussion to personally significant questions, like "What can we as individuals living in another country possibly do to help the victims of these violations?"

The group could then discuss strategies such as joining a local human rights group or writing to politicians and the press.

Posters, photographs, symbols, cartoons, and children's artwork also make excellent discussion starters. In the following sections we include some graphics we have used, with examples of questions and answers.

An Environmental Example from Greenpeace

This photograph of a Greenpeace campaigner holding a dead baby dolphin was circulated by Greenpeace as part of a recent fundraising drive. The dolphin, caught by Japanese fishers in the Tasman Sea in

© Greenpeace/Dorreboom

Baby dolphin killed by drift-nets.

January 1990, was one of many killed by drift-nets intended to catch tuna. Questions like these could be asked to stimulate discussion about the disastrous ecological effects of drift-net fishing.

What do you see in this photograph? There's a woman on a boat holding a dead baby dolphin.

What killed the dolphin? Drift-net fishing.

What is drift-net fishing? Huge fishing trawlers use drift-nets to catch tuna and squid. The nets are made of plastic monofilament and measure 14 meters deep and up to 56 kilometers long.

Why is drift-net fishing so bad for the environment? Greenpeace refers to drift-net fishing as "stripmining the seas." Apart from their enormous size, drift-nets are so sheer that even the sensitive sonar of dolphins cannot detect them. So the nets trap and kill nearly every large fish or mammal in their path, including dolphins, seabirds, turtles, sharks, and even whales.

Why is the woman holding the dead baby dolphin? Greenpeace wants to use this photo to inform people all over the world about what is happening to marine life because of drift-net fishing, so she is posing for the photo. (With older children, you may want to discuss the power of visual images, how organizations use images for their own purposes such as advertising, propaganda, etc.)

How do you think she feels? She looks sad because it is so unfair that the dolphin had to die this way. Perhaps she feels upset and angry, and determined to do something to stop this senseless killing of marine life.

What is the *Rainbow Warrior*? It is the name of the vessel Greenpeace activists have used in many of their water-based campaigns to end whaling, water pollution, and drift-net fishing.

What is Greenpeace doing to stop the killing of dolphins? They have launched a massive, international public education campaign, and have lobbied the United Nations to pass a resolution banning drift-nets in 1992.

How can people like us help stop the unnecessary killing of dolphins and other marine life? We can support environmental organizations fighting to save marine life from the drift-nets; join consumer boycotts of tuna that is not labeled "dolphin-friendly"; educate others about this issue; write letters of protest to government leaders, especially of countries that still use drift-nets, such as France, Taiwan, Japan, and South Korea.

A Peace-related Example from Earth Beat Press

This graphic is from the cover of *We Can Do It! A Peace Book for Kids of All Ages* by Morrison, Dehr, and Bazar, 1985 ($3 postage paid, Earth Beat Press, Box 33852, Station D, Vancouver, BC, Canada V6J 4L6). We use it to start discussions about caring for people all over the world and for the earth.

What do you see in this drawing? Happy children holding up the world; children of many nationalities touching the earth; girls and boys and younger and older children all cooperating and being equals.

What does the picture mean to you? It means that people of different backgrounds can get along and make peace in the world; building peace is everyone's responsibility; there are no political boundaries in this drawing, and there should be no barriers between people, either; peace begins with the children; we should work together to save the earth; we can all do something positive for the earth; if we look after the earth it will look after us; it's fun to be an earth saver; it's our responsibility to do something for the earth.

How do you think these children feel, and why? They look very happy, even though they have a big job to do and a very responsible one. "Many hands make light work," and they are all good friends, so peace-building is fun, not a burden. They are feeling positive and powerful; they are even wearing shirts that say "We can do it!"

What kind of a world would this be if everyone cared for each other and for the earth like these children do? It would be a world worth living in!

How can we get together with other children to work for peace and to help care for the earth? See Appendix 2 for a list of relevant organizations.

A Human Rights Example from Amnesty International

This symbol is used by Amnesty International, the human rights organization that works for the release of prisoners of conscience, in the Prisoners of the Month section of *Amnesty International Bulletin.* We ask questions like the following to initiate a discussion about human rights violations and the work of Amnesty International.

What do you see in this picture? A dove is flying away from broken chains.

What does it mean to you? Who might the bird represent? The dove is a symbol of peace, so maybe peace is being given a chance to work freely, unhindered. It might also mean that peace, justice, and good have triumphed over evil, that people who have been locked

Graphic used by Amnesty International.

away have been freed, or that people who have been oppressed have been liberated. The bird might even represent a great idea that has been censored or suppressed for too long.

How do you think the bird feels? Birds love to be free to fly, so it must feel very happy to be liberated after being held captive.

How does this picture make you feel? It makes us feel optimistic, happy, relieved, free, excited, like there is so much that can be achieved with liberty!

If the dove represents a prisoner of conscience (explain that concept if necessary), how might the chains have been broken? Maybe the government that imprisoned the person has been overthrown. Perhaps the prisoner escaped, or has died and is thus spiritually freed. Maybe the authorities realized they were being unfair and decided to release the person. Or perhaps they were forced to release the person because of public pressure. (Flesh out this idea: what kinds of people can bring pressure to bear on unjust authorities? Family members are often at great risk of being detained or "disappeared" themselves, and can't always speak out against injustice. So it is up to prominent citizens, clerics, journalists, international politicians and diplomats, and ordinary people like Amnesty International supporters from other countries to protest on behalf of prisoners of conscience.)

What can we do to help people who have been imprisoned for their beliefs? Through international organizations like Amnesty International, we can give money to support the people who research and publicize what happens to prisoners of conscience all over the world. We can also write letters or send telegrams to the relevant authorities calling for the release of prisoners. We can donate money and materials to help the families of such prisoners, who are often left without income. We can be active in helping local refugees, because many refugees have fled their countries after being harassed, threatened, or imprisoned for their beliefs. We can keep ourselves informed about human rights issues and abuses, speak out against such abuses, and educate others in turn.

STORIES, POEMS, SONGS, AND CHANTS

It can be tempting to include a favorite song or story in a session, but if you want it to serve as a discussion starter, consider its *relevance*. Will the song (or poem, story, or chant) in fact stimulate participants to discuss their thoughts and feelings about the topic? If it is only vaguely related, use something else to stimulate discussion initially, and perhaps include the song later in the session to reinforce a concept, introduce variety, or change the pace.

Teaching children a simple song in another language (or how to greet or count to five) can be a fun way of introducing an international education theme. Folktales from other cultures or picture books featuring children in another country are also useful. The book by Condon and McGinnis (1988) is an excellent source for simple chants children can say or sing to accompany activities like puppet shows and dressing up.

Try asking questions for children to consider before you read a story or poem, or before singing or playing a song (e.g., "Why is the bear sad? Who is most helpful when she feels sad?"). This focuses their attention and provides a preview of the material, though you should obviously not give away the climax. These same questions can then be used to initiate discussion afterward. Once the group is warmed up, you can move on to more personal reactions (e.g., "What would you have done if you were the cow in that story?" or "How did you feel when . . . ?") and, if appropriate, suggestions for action ("What can we do to . . . ?"). With young children or when dealing with strong emotions, we ask them to act out their feelings instead of discussing them.

This poem we wrote has been a useful discussion starter about war toys and their effects on our thinking about conflict resolution and violence in society.

Suburban War

There's a war being waged in the suburbs,
There's a battle that's raging right here.
There is anger and hatred,
        violence and fears.
There is running and shouting,
        shooting and tears.
There's a war going on in the suburbs.

But relax, just calm down.
It's all "fun," don't you see?
Just a game:
Guns are toys.
And the soldiers,
Girls and boys.

Appendix 1 lists resources that we and other educators have found most useful as discussion starters. Pacijou (listed in Appendix 2) has copies of poetry written by French-speaking children.

MOVIES, VIDEOS, AND SLIDES

Visual media can be very powerful discussion starters when sensitively and skillfully used. The National Film Board of Canada's catalogue of movies and videos is an excellent resource for educators (see Appendix 2 for their address); readers in other countries can find out about their own local organizations that lend educational films and other media. Amnesty International also has films and videos available (see Appendix 2). Mainstream movies with alternative heroes (nonviolent, handicapped, or of different races or cultures) are also excellent. Consider *Awakenings, Cry Freedom, Children of a Lesser God, The Mission, Romero, Gandhi,* and *Dances with Wolves,* among many others.

Learners often put their minds into "neutral" when the lights are dimmed and the projector or video begins. We try to counter the passive role into which these media usually place people by preparing viewers beforehand and discussing what they saw, thought, and felt immediately afterward.

For example, we once showed a movie about how the seasons affect a tree and the organisms that live in and around it. The learning group included children as young as 5 years and preteens. When we previewed the movie (an essential step before you can decide whether to use it or not), we decided that there was enough to hold the attention of everyone in the group, provided they were prepared beforehand. So we asked younger children to watch for and later list all the animals, birds, and insects they saw in the movie, and to note what they were doing to survive during the different seasons. The older children were asked to concentrate on and later summarize and explain some of the more technical details about photosynthesis, and so on. This division of labor worked well: even the youngest, squirmiest members concentrated during the twenty-minute movie, and the discussion afterward was lively. The young ones enjoyed "educating" the older members, who had been concentrating on other aspects of the movie.

OTHER VISUAL AND AUDIO AIDS

Depending on the topic and the ages of the children, we use aids like maps, globes, posters, and tape recordings to start discussions. Often the most effective aids are real objects, like toys and clothing from other countries, or food and eating utensils from other cultures.

Preschoolers love globes: they're colorful, feel good to touch, and spin!

Serge Marsolais painted a huge world map, measuring 9 feet by 12 feet, for the international education sessions he facilitated at the YMCA day camps. The children were impressed by the sheer size of the map, and it was an effective aid. Depending on the ages of the children with whom you work, you might consider asking them to help you design and make some of the aids for future sessions.

A bulletin board with news clippings is also useful. We ask children to bring clippings related to our topics, and after they summarize them, we pin up all the positive clippings (say, about peace, disarmament, or environmental protection) on one side of the board, opposite the negative ones (about war, the arms race, or environmental destruction). The children soon see that bad news makes good news: negative stories get much more coverage. So our challenge as activists is to think of ways to keep our causes in the media. With older children, this exercise can be expanded to include critical discussion of the media, how the news is made, whose views are given exposure, bias and censorship in reporting, and so on. They may also want to discuss how they can help to get more media exposure for causes to which they feel committed. For example, children can get good coverage if they organize and publicize community peace ceremonies or protests; if they win poetry, essay, or art competitions; and if they write letters to newspapers.

QUESTIONS

In some circumstances, a simple, clear, provocative question is still the best way to generate discussion, especially with older children and teens. For example, late in 1990, following Iraq's invasion of Kuwait, the question, "Should Western countries be sending troops to the Persian Gulf?" was guaranteed to stimulate a heated debate.

BRAINSTORMING

This is an excellent way for a group to start a discussion by generating ideas that can be reordered, sorted, and sifted out later. Brainstorming starts with a question, e.g., "How can we make people more aware of the dangers of nuclear weapons?" "What are the effects of radiation on the human body?" "Why are the rainforests being destroyed?" Someone, preferably a group member rather than the animator, writes down all the ideas that participants call out. Don't allow argument or censorship of ideas—they inhibit participants, interrupt the flow of ideas, and block the process. Even apparently outrageous ideas are included and given equal consideration; often, such ideas suggest the most innovative solutions to a problem. If a contribution is factually inappropriate, wait to explain why and eliminate it during the second part of the exercise. Keep a brisk pace, getting all ideas down on paper quickly. When the group has run dry, start the next stage: reorder, categorize, prioritize, and eliminate ideas.

We have enjoyed using a combination of brainstorming and poetry composition; see "Composing and Writing" in Chapter 1 for a discussion of cooperative poetry.

Children enjoy brainstorming once they get used to the unusual conditions. At first, many can't resist censoring each other's contributions. Even in groups of mixed ages, the youngest members get excited by the fast pace and the nonjudgmental atmosphere, and contribute their ideas. Seeing the secretary write down their point boosts their confidence. Even when they are too young to read, children understand the social significance of having their ideas recorded on paper.

QUOTATIONS

A controversial or eloquent quotation can stimulate a good discussion, especially with older children and teens who are used to debating issues. Here are some examples; also see the book *Seeds of Peace* by Larson and Micheels-Cyrus (1987).

- The money needed to provide adequate food, water, education, health care, and housing for everyone in the world is estimated at $17 billion per year . . . about as much as the world spends on arms every ten days. — *World Bank*

- Peace is not something you *wish* for; it's something you *make*, something you *do*, something you *are*, and something you *give away*. — *Robert Fulghum*

- The earth is one, but the world is not. — *Brundtland Commission*

- Inequality is the planet's biggest environmental problem. — *Gro Brundtland*

- The world has enough for everyone's need but not for everyone's greed. — *Theodore Roszak*

- The earth is not being destroyed by industrialists alone; it is being destroyed by every consumer. — *Wendell Berry*

- The next step should be backward—backward to a new place. . . . The only sensible thing to do at the edge of a precipice is to step back. — *Kirkpatrick Sale*

- If everybody in the world did what I was doing, what would the environment be like? — *Ralph Nader*

Chapter 3

Ice Breaking and Community Building

In each class or course, a unique pattern of circumstances, pressures,
customs, opinions, and work styles [emerges] which suffuse[s] the
teaching and learning that occur there.
— *Parlett and Dearden, 1977:14–15*

*   *   *   *   *

It's the first meeting of the peace club. The young children sit stiffly
in a circle on the floor, with us, cross-legged, between them. They look
a bit apprehensive, having no idea yet what to expect, or what is
expected of them. So far, they have only introduced themselves by
name.

We smile and say, "We are going to pass a secret message around the
circle. Each person should listen carefully to the whispered message
and then pass it on." At the very mention of words like "secret" and
"whisper," the children get excited. They lean forward, eyes shining,
smiling, waiting for their turn to hear the message.

"Psst psst psst."

"What? I didn't hear properly," says Maki.

"Psst psst psst."

"Oh, okay." Maki grins, turns to Pierre, and whispers, "Psst psst psst."

As the message goes around, an almost palpable change of mood
occurs. The physical closeness demanded by the act of whispering
loosens them up. The tickling feeling in the ear causes many to squirm
or giggle. The excitement builds as the message passes from one child
to the next.

Finally, the last person repeats what she has heard out loud: "I am
a member of the world family."

This message is the theme for the day's international education
session. One of us leans forward to ask, "What do you think that
message means?" There is thus a natural flow from this ice-breaking
exercise into the rest of the session, and because the children are more
relaxed now than before, they participate actively in all the learning
activities.

*   *   *   *   *

BREAKING THE ICE

When a new group comes together, members often feel unsure, even
anxious. They keep their defenses up, wondering, "What are these other
people like? Will I like them, and they me? Will I fit in here? Can I be
myself?" It is as if a layer of ice is covering the group.

Ice breaking is essential in situations where you want participants to take initiative, develop leadership skills, share responsibility for what happens in the group, actively participate, have fun, and learn not only from you but from others and their interactions with others. It encourages people in the group to relax and get to know each other.

If you will be with the same group over a long period, you may want to spend relatively more time breaking the ice and building a cooperative learning community. On the other hand, if you are giving a lecture or formal presentation to a large audience, expecting little or no participation from them, there is less need to break the ice, though the five or ten minutes you spend breaking the ice initially will allow the remaining time to be used more productively.

An animator's job is to help members break the ice so they can feel comfortable relating to others and participating to their full potential. Many educators say that they want learners to participate actively, but they don't *take the time* to break the ice that effectively prevents this from happening. Ice seldom melts spontaneously; it needs a source of heat! Warmth from the animator's own enthusiastic approach and from some specially designed, ice-breaking exercises are usually needed.

The ice is thickest when a group first meets, but it also reforms after a tea or lunch break, after the group has dispersed to work on individual projects or in small groups, when a new member or latecomer joins, when a visitor or guest speaker attends, when participants get tired, or after an unpleasant or stressful interaction. Are there other ice-forming times you've experienced as a participant or animator?

Here are some descriptions of ice breakers we have used. Some are designed to introduce group members to each other; others, to introduce a new topic or theme; and still others, to energize participants.

ICE BREAKERS TO INTRODUCE PARTICIPANTS

What makes an effective ice breaker? We like activities that are short, fun, attention-getting, and involve the active participation of all members. Especially with children, effective ice breaking often involves doing something active (like clapping, miming, running in a circle, bending and stretching, or dancing), or noisy (like reciting, chanting, singing, making music, or shouting), or both.

Some educators start each session the same way, with children reciting a poem, chant, or motto and acting out the movements, for example, or by singing a club song or greeting each other in a foreign language. Such repetition can give children a sense of belonging and focus them on being truly present in the group. But this type of beginning could become an empty ritual if not accompanied by other intentional ice-breaking and community-building activities.

Appendix 1 lists some of the resources that have stimulated our thinking about ice breaking. Your own adaptations of exercises will be most applicable; only you know exactly what your needs are.

When people first come together, they need to get to know other group members. For a short, one-off session, simply learning the names of fellow participants is a good start; we do more detailed introductions if the group is going to work together over time.

The Clapping Circle

Children and animator sit cross-legged in a tight circle on the floor. Everyone claps hands twice, claps on knees twice, and then listens while the first person says their name and age, school, country of birth, or other information. Clapping then continues and the others introduce themselves in turn. This breaks the ice, helps members learn each others' names, and gives a quick overview of their backgrounds. It's a good exercise for groups with very young members who cannot write their own names on name tags.

Cooperative Name Tags

Have large cardboard name tags, pencils, and colored pens or paints available. As participants arrive, ask them to decorate a border on a name tag, perhaps using their favorite peace symbols, and to write their name in pencil on the back. When everyone has done a border, the tags are pooled and people each take one (if you choose your own border, put it back and take another) and write their name (large, so it will be legible from across the circle) inside the border. They then look at the penciled name on the back of their tags, meet the person who colored their border, and those two become partners or "first friends" for the session; they sit next to each other, work in pairs for subsequent activities, and so on. Use the name tags in subsequent sessions until everyone knows each other's names.

The Name Game

Think of a word that describes how you feel (or what kind of person you are, or the kind of person you'd like to be, or whatever) and that begins with the same letter as your name. Going round the circle, let people introduce themselves (Naughty Nancy, Peaceful Patrick) and say something about why they chose that word. Participants learning many new names can often remember the descriptive word someone used, which informs them of the first letter of the name, which in turn makes remembering the name much easier.

Introductions in Pairs

This is an excellent ice breaker, but it takes from one-half to one hour, depending on group size and how much detailed information participants share. It is not suitable for groups with more than twelve or fourteen members, because the group round at the end takes too long for people to concentrate.

In the short version, participants pair off and interview their partners to learn their names, ages, numbers of siblings, schools, hobbies, what first got them interested in joining the peace group, and so on. After each person has interviewed and been interviewed (about ten minutes—leave more time for older children and teens, less for younger ones), the group reassembles and each person introduces her or his partner. A friendly atmosphere often develops as people say, "My new friend is . . ." or "My partner. . . ."

In the long version of this exercise, the animator first asks the group to brainstorm what items they want to include in the interviewing list, apart from the usual biographical details about name, age, and so on. Teens might be interested in hearing about what others in the group think about a current news issue, or what they are planning to do once they have finished school. Including this step in the exercise takes more time, but it shows participants that you are open to their ideas, that you are not merely going to dictate to the group. This exercise thus not only helps to break ice—it can be a significant community-building exercise, too.

What are the advantages of using introductions in pairs, rather than each person introducing herself? First, everyone can warm up while relating in a nonthreatening, one-on-one situation. Second, people often share things about themselves in pairs that they would not normally say in a new group; this creates a sense of intimacy at the outset. Third, shy participants often find it less threatening to introduce a partner than themselves in the big group. And finally, confident members who might be long-winded about themselves don't get too talkative when introducing a partner.

Spin the Pen

This can be used to start a second or subsequent session. Sitting in a tight circle, each person takes a turn to spin a pen. When it points to someone, the spinner tries to remember that person's name and perhaps other biographical details. If s/he can't remember, others quickly help out. Keep the mood light and jovial to avoid having people feel embarrassed by their memory lapses.

SETTING THE SCENE FOR A NEW TOPIC OR THEME

These exercises are economical; they help to break the ice at the same time as they introduce a new theme. This gets participants thinking about the content of the day's discussions and activities.

Secret Message

This is the exercise we described at the start of this chapter, when a whispered message gets passed around the circle. We have used it to introduce an international education theme ("I am a member of the world family") and an environmental theme ("I am a child of the earth"). Younger children need short, clear messages; older ones can be challenged by a longer one ("I am a child of the earth, and all living organisms are children of the earth"). A line from a well-known song or poem makes a good message, as does a famous or challenging quotation. Once the message has been made public by the last person in the circle, ask participants what the message means to them, and the discussion flows naturally into the new topic.

Foreign Words

Participants need to do some preparation for their next session. For example, ask them to write down the word for peace (or love, cooperation, justice, forest, or whatever your theme is) in a foreign language and to bring it to the next meeting. This preparation often serves to involve others in their families, and the words can be used in subsequent craft activities to make murals, collages, or flags. To break the ice next time, go round the circle and ask each person to say the word s/he chose. If pronunciation is a problem, they can show the written form of the word. Others can guess which language it is, and locate the country on a map or globe.

Graphics

If you have a poster, picture, photo, or graphic symbol that relates to your theme, start a session by showing it and asking participants what they see or how it makes them feel. Give some time for people to experience the graphic before beginning a group round and discussion. (We also mentioned graphics as discussion starters in the previous chapter.)

ENERGIZING PARTICIPANTS

During long sessions and in groups with young members who lose concentration quickly, try including short, active exercises to wake up participants and regenerate waning energies.

Some animators use conventional party games like Simple Simon Says or Hot Potato; we prefer noncompetitive games and exercises, where the whole group works together in harmony. (See Chapter 1 for a discussion of cooperative games.)

Try activities like singing, dancing, listening to lively music, yoga-type exercises, meditation, or even aerobics. A break and change of pace does wonders when spirits are low.

Breaking the ice is one of the first steps in the long and challenging process of building and maintaining a cooperative learning climate. But if you want members of the group to relate easily, to feel empowered by their participation, and to learn effectively, there is more work ahead: community building.

COMMUNITY BUILDING

*   *   *   *   *

About half an hour into the group's first meeting, we become aware of some group-process problems. Older children are dominating; some of the boys often interrupt when a girl is talking; one person sniggers rudely when she disagrees with what someone else says; and two of the younger members have just started a disruptive game of tickling and tugging.

Time to negotiate some ground rules!

"Everyone freeze, please! Stop everything, let's stay exactly where we are and examine what is happening. What is going on, and how do you feel about how we are all working together so far?"

The children make a chorus: "Jean-Claude and Jamie are playing on the floor"; "Penny keeps leaning on me"; "Maki doesn't let me finish speaking"; "Anita keeps laughing at what we say." We hear people out, defusing any unnecessarily harsh accusations and asking them how it feels to be laughed at, ignored, or interrupted. This helps participants become more aware of their own actions and those of others, and also of the effects their actions have on others.

When appropriate, we use "big words" like *discrimination, sexism, racism, cooperation, compromise,* and *disruption,* explaining what each means. (Later, we smile to hear them telling each other not to be sexist, etc.) Finally, we tell the group we want them to help generate a list of ground rules that we will all respect so the group can work together effectively and enjoyably. Their commitment to ground rules will be much greater if they themselves negotiate them, and the process of negotiation—a crucial part of peacekeeping in any real-world setting—will be a major learning experience, too.

The children work in small groups to brainstorm ideas for the list. This ensures that everyone gets a chance to voice their ideas. Too often, in a large group it is only the outspoken, confident, and older members who make themselves heard. When splitting the group, we divide the shyer and younger members between the groups and usually separate siblings and close friends; they bring a long, not necessarily helpful history of interaction patterns. We ask one person to make notes, one to act as facilitator, and one to be in charge of process in the small group, ensuring that everyone gets a fair chance to talk, disagree, and contribute constructively.

Back in the large group, we pool ideas, asking an older child to keep notes on newsprint. Why should a child act as secretary? The person standing and holding the pen or chalk is in a position of power over others in the group. We find it liberating for participants to take turns in that position. Some of the items on the final list are given below.

- We are all equal here.
- We are here to help each other.
- We all have some good (and not-so-good!) ideas to contribute.
- We can disagree with someone without fighting and being rude or unkind.

We are often touched by the fairness, depth of insight, and maturity that even young children can show when they contribute to lists like this. We use the same words the children used, rather than rephrasing their ideas and thereby taking over the process to some extent. Freire (1970) makes this point in relation to "using the words" of adult learners in literacy groups.

Impressed by their cooperatively generated list, Penny volunteers to type it so they can all get a copy. We thank her, ask others if they would like that (they say "yes"), and congratulate Penny on her good idea and initiative. After this session, several of the children enthusiastically tell us and their parents how much fun they are having in the peace club, and especially how grown-up they feel to have a say in what happens.

*   *   *   *   *

What Is a Cooperative Learning Community?

We use the term *learning community* to refer to the following aspects of an educational situation.

- **Social relations**—What is the nature of interactions between learners and educators, and among learners themselves?

- **Psychological conditions**—What is the level of mutual respect, trust, and acceptance in the group? Do participants feel safe enough to let down their defenses and be themselves?

- **Intellectual norms**—Are learners free to introduce new content issues? Are some ideas or emotions censored? Does the animator show respect for the intellectual abilities of all participants? Are dissent, conflict, and challenge encouraged or disapproved of?

- **Administrative set-up**—Are plans rigid or flexible? Are decisions made democratically by the group or arbitrarily by the educator?

For our purposes, a *cooperative learning community* is one in which children can relax, be themselves, and have fun while being challenged to extend their thinking, help others, and share responsibility for what happens in the group. Participants feel accepted, empowered, and free to participate to their fullest potential. There is a sense of belonging to a supportive learning community. Participants feel interconnected, in dialogue with others, open to learning, and ready for action, *not* alienated, alarmed, or alone. Building such a community often involves a fundamental redistribution of power and a redefinition of roles, since few learners (or educators) are used to functioning in a cooperative community.

While a cooperative learning community is conducive to any kind of learning, educators concerned about social responsibility should take special care to build such a community. It is illogical and unfair to expect children to learn about peace, love, respect, justice, and cooperation in a group that lacks these very features.

Apart from facilitating learning, a cooperative community encourages children to develop leadership skills, behave more assertively in a group, respect the rights and ideas of others, take risks and try out new behaviors in a psychologically safe setting, work constructively as a member of a team, and use conflict creatively to extend their thinking.

BUILDING A COOPERATIVE LEARNING COMMUNITY

Animators tend to take for granted that a sense of community will automatically develop once the group assembles. This seldom happens without the conscious intervention of a skilled facilitator. Building a cooperative community requires directed effort, and maintaining it is an ongoing task throughout the life of the group. Breaking the ice and keeping it broken is part of this process, but not sufficient in itself.

No group of children can be expected to be attentive—let alone cooperative—for long if certain basic conditions for learning are lacking. For example, they need to be engaged in active and challenging work, experience frequent changes of pace, be exposed to a range of activities and visual or other aids, have frequent breaks, be allowed to move and preferably run or play outdoors between sessions, eat a snack during a long session, and have free access to a bathroom. What other basic conditions to facilitate learning do you try to meet?

Once these basic conditions have been met, an animator's own attitude and personality probably have the greatest influence on the learning community in a group.

> The beliefs, feelings and assumptions of teachers are the air of a learning environment; they determine the quality of life within it. When the air is polluted, the student is poisoned, unless, of course, [s/]he holds [her/]his breath. (Postman and Weingartner, 1969:43)

Animators can literally transform a learning group if they are

- self-confident, and therefore not clinging to a role in which they exercise arbitrary authority over others,

- enthusiastic about both the *content* of their work and the *process* of working with children,

- accepting and affirming,

- warm and friendly,

- fun-loving and playful, and

- generous with praise.

These qualities make for a learning climate in which children are free to learn, grow, and have fun in the process. Rogers (1961, 1983) emphasizes the need for educators to be "genuine" or "real;" to be *themselves* rather than playing the role of teacher.

Community-building Exercises and Activities

We have discussed the need to include ice-breaking exercises. Community building also needs intentional intervention. Examples include:

- dealing with group-process problems openly, negotiating with participants rather than imposing rules;

- encouraging open, challenging, but nonthreatening communication;

- breaking into small groups for some tasks;

- using the words of participants rather than rephrasing ideas;

- asking a group member to keep notes on the board;

- praising participants without patronizing them;

- organizing occasional social events like picnics, parties, and hikes, where animators and learners can relate in a relaxed setting away from the classroom with its connotations of power and powerlessness;

- using specially designed trust- and relationship-building exercises (see Hope and Timmel, 1984);

- building the self-esteem of participants, since people who feel good about themselves are more likely to cooperate and enjoy others (for ideas see Park, 1985, 1988; Park and Park, 1990a, b);

- playing cooperative rather than competitive games;

- using culturally and age-appropriate physical contact between animators and learners;

- including learners in making decisions about the topics to be included and methods to be used in future sessions; and

- consulting group members about administrative decisions in a democratic fashion.

Resolving Conflict and Keeping the Peace

Conflict and disagreement are inevitable and not necessarily undesirable in human affairs. Our challenge is neither to eliminate nor gloss over them, but to help children learn skills to resolve conflict constructively, creatively, and cooperatively.

Use conflicts that arise in the group as learning opportunities. Help the children step back from their emotional baggage, listen carefully to each other, try to see things from the other's perspective, state their own positions clearly and assertively but not aggressively, and remain open and flexible in order to find mutually agreeable solutions. With practice, they realize that conflicts can be creatively resolved in ways in which everybody wins and feels good, instead of in win-lose ways that leave someone feeling bad. Links can be drawn to other situations where conflict is often unimaginatively tackled by quick resort to violence, coercion, abuse, and domination.

Park and Park (1990a:25–30) describe a Peace Train exercise that teaches conflict-resolution principles to children. The carriages on the train are

1. Stop—don't get drawn into an argument or fight;
2. Identify the problem;
3. Generate solutions, even violent ones;
4. Check the feelings each solution would elicit in yourself and others; and
5. Negotiate a resolution.

A regular forum for participants to discuss problems is an essential part of peacekeeping. A weekly class or family meeting gives people a chance to talk in a respectful and controled setting, and often prevents negative feelings from erupting into abusive or violent outbursts.

Disciplining children is a thorny issue for many adults. We include children when generating lists of ground rules. At home and at work we find this prevents and deals with most problems. Also, we often rely on peer pressure to bring a child's disruptive behavior into line, rather than playing a disciplinary role.

> [When Maxine did something that upset other children] it was the teacher who responded, not the victim, and so Maxine could not find out the meaning of her action among her peers. Nor could that long and subtle chain of children's reactions – with all their surprising turns of patience and generosity – even begin to take shape. . . .
>
> [Later, in a different school, the teacher did not intervene in children's arguments and Maxine was forced to face the true consequences of her actions.] While she can absorb endless numbers of demerits, endless hours of detention, endless homilies and rebukes, she must pay attention to this massed voice of her own group. She needs them. They are her play-mates. (Dennison, in Holt, 1970:49, 50)

If you don't immediately intervene when a child becomes disruptive, members of the group soon take responsibility for keeping the peace. A simple "cut that out—I can't hear!" from a friend is often much more effective than adult appeals, warnings, and threats. Initially the children may ask you to intervene: "Please tell Maki to stop leaning on me." We refer the problem back: "Why don't you ask him, Jane?" By now, all eyes in the room are on Maki and Jane, as she asks him to quit. Quite often, others who have previously been leaned on (or whatever) come to Jane's support: "Yeah, it's irritating when you do that!" After a short while, children get into the habit of dealing with their own problems without trying to involve us first. We much prefer that, since it's less stressful than our having to feel solely responsible for keeping the peace. And it allows our relationships with each child to be less affected by their interactions with each other.

When we are in doubt about the most appropriate way to respond to a difficult situation, we use what Kendall calls the "adult test."

> Whenever you are not sure how you should respond to your child's actions, apply the Adult Test. Ask yourself, "What would I do if this were an adult?" . . . If your friend visits your house and breaks a glass by mistake, do you shout "you clumsy idiot!" at her and shove her out of your way? On the contrary, you understand that she did not intend to break the glass, you allay her feelings of guilt and help her clean up the mess. If she broke the glass because she had never seen one before and presumed that it would behave in the same way as a plastic tumbler, you might take a little time to point out the difference. You should relate to your child exactly as you would to your friend. . . . Making allowance for their lack of experience, we should treat children exactly as we treat adults. (Kendall, 1983:20)

Kendall takes a firm position with which many may not agree. What do you think of her ideas? If you agree in principle, how consistent is your practice? Some people react against what she says, thinking that children will run riot if they are treated as adults. But few of us would stand for an adult friend, say, coming into the kitchen and smashing our crockery just for fun. We would take steps to stop such destruction; we would set limits on the person's behavior. Children need limits too. But how those limits are negotiated and applied differs considerably depending on whether you approach children as undisciplined terrors or as your friends. So neither Kendall nor we are advocating an abrogation of responsibility here; adults obviously have to set clear limits on behavior that is unacceptable (e.g., if it is potentially dangerous or damaging to property, or if it infringes on the rights of others). But as we have said, children can often help set those limits themselves, monitor their own behavior accordingly, and when necessary enforce the limits by putting pressure on their peers.

As parents and as educators, we are amazed by how positively children—even very young ones—respond to being treated with the same respect and sensitivity that we give to adults. We also feel liberated when we stop playing the controling role in typically authoritarian parent-child and teacher-pupil relationships.

Chapter 4
Session Plans

> To be fully alive and meaningful, a training course . . . needs to be
> redesigned not only for each area and set of conditions
> where it is taught, but each time it is taught.
> — *Werner and Bower, 1982*

PLANNING A PROVISIONAL PROGRAM

What are the steps in planning a provisional program? We stress
provisional because no educational program should be carved in stone;
rather, it should be flexible, dynamic, and responsive to the children's
interests and changing needs.

Analyze Your Situation

Educators working for peace, justice, equality, and freedom must
first analyze and become critically aware of the violence, injustice,
inequality, and oppression that surround and confound us. A careful
situational analysis clarifies the needs we should address and allows us
to plan relevant programs, anticipate and avoid obstacles, and perhaps
even become more open to progressive action.

Some questions to ask yourself as you analyze your situation include

- How does the social-economic-political context affect
  me and the learners with whom I work?

- How will the sector (e.g., educational, health,
  commercial) and subsector (e.g., primary or
  secondary education, formal or nonformal education)
  within which I work influence me? For example,
  where does the power in my sector lie? Where does
  the funding come from? Whose support must I get
  before I innovate with education for social
  responsibility?

- Who am I educating (boys and/or girls, upper- and
  middle-class children or working-class ones,
  English- or French-speaking children, children of
  established families or new immigrants)? Am I
  satisfied with the current situation?

- What are the ages, interests, and past experiences of
  the children? Are these taken into account in
  educational planning?

- What is my main objective in working with the children? What do I expect them to be able to do afterward? Are my expectations realistic, considering the time and resources available, their ages, and so on?

- Who are the most appropriate role models for the children?

For strategies to help learners and educators make more critical situation analyses, see Hammond and Collins, 1991 (79–83).

Determine Learning Priorities

As a program developer, you will have some ideas about issues you want to raise with the children. Possibilities might include world peace, nuclear power and nuclear weapons, military spending, the arms race and disarmament, military conversion, global and local environmental problems, cross-cultural and interracial tolerance, or human rights abuses. But the specific examples you use and the priorities you set will depend on

- The interests and backgrounds of the children concerned,

- Local circumstances (e.g., Are you working in a neighborhood where racial tensions have been increasing? Is language or religious intolerance a major issue in your area?), and

- Current events.

Set Objectives

> If you're not sure where you're going, you're liable to end up someplace else—and not even know it. (Mager, 1962:vii)

Setting objectives encourages us to choose appropriate learning and teaching strategies. We distinguish between objectives set for each of the three learning domains: cognitive (knowledge), affective (attitudes), and psychomotor (skills), and try to keep a balance between the three domains in our work. Too many programs focus on the cognitive domain, and within that, low-level cognitive functions like memorizing and simple recall are often stressed above high-level ones like analysis, problem-solving, synthesis, and evaluation. When trying to communicate a message with an emotional component (e.g., respect for the whales, or concern for the homeless or victims of torture), we use evocative discussion starters like stories, poetry, music, or pictures. These involve and engage children more deeply than a simple presentation of information could ever do.

When we first started using learning objectives, we wrote detailed ones that specified the *action* a learner should be able to take by the end of the session, the *content* and the *conditions* under which learning should occur, and the evaluation *criteria*. See the objective below, for example.

> **Conditions:** By the end of this session, having taken the pretest quiz, having listened to the relevant read-aloud extracts from *Good Planets Are Hard to Find*, and having participated in a group discussion, each child will be able to
> **Action:** make a list of
> **Content:** at least five behavioral changes they themselves can make to reduce permanently the use of paper in their homes.
> **Criteria:** The listed changes must be both relevant to paper-reduction as well as feasible, economical, and safe. Examples include using handkerchiefs instead of Kleenex, using reusable plastic plates instead of paper plates, reusing old computer paper for art projects, and cleaning up with kitchen cloths instead of paper towels.

Later, we found we could use a shorthand version to guide our practice, and we often set session objectives rather than learning objectives. Given our preference for involving children in planning, a session objective may simply be to help children choose and plan for their next topic. Try experimenting with different types of objectives until you find something that suits you.

Critics of learning objectives say that their use makes education restrictive and inflexible, that they dehumanize the essentially human pursuits of learning and teaching. Proponents, on the other hand, say objectives provide a crucial map for both learners and teachers, and that publicly stated objectives increase teacher accountability. Having considered the pros and cons, what do you think?

Plan Your Sessions

Setting objectives is really the first step in planning each session. If you like, you can then draft a detailed session plan, specifying what learning activities and media you will use, how long each activity should last, and how you will evaluate the session and the children's learning. We always make a session plan in advance; it's reassuring and gives us confidence about our work. But at the same time, we know that a session is seldom implemented exactly as planned. Sometimes one activity takes too long, or is omitted because it just doesn't feel right for this group on this day. So we follow our gut feelings and stay flexible, even when we feel particularly committed to specific exercises or activities.

We aim for a sense of coherence and wholeness in each session by using activities that build logically on each other and on previous sessions, and that have a balance of emotional, practical, and intellectual content. Disparate, unrelated activities to fill the time have no place in a program that respects its participants. With young children, we also try to balance quiet, sedentary activities with active, physical ones.

We start planning for a session by doing a detailed situation analysis. In the section about program planning above, we discussed the need for macro-level situation analysis, in which we consider the social-economic-political context in which we are working, and the forces operating within our particular sector. Some micro-level aspects of the situation to be considered during session planning include

- Target group analysis: How old are the children? How many in the group? What past experience and prior knowledge do they have relating to the topic? What are their interests?

- Duration of the session.

- Venue: Indoors or outdoors or both? Will participants sit on the floor or on chairs? Is there desk space for each member?

- Available resources: Movie projector and screen, blinds for windows, books, artifacts from other countries, art and craft supplies.

- Time of day: With young children especially, morning sessions can be more intense than afternoon ones when they are tired. The darkness of evening or night sessions often adds a special magic that makes learning more memorable.

- Feedback from previous sessions with this group.

We determine learning priorities and set objectives based on the situation analysis. Then we choose appropriate learning and teaching methods and media for ice breaking, community building, and achieving content-related objectives. Estimating how much time is needed for each activity is another task. A common error to avoid is the use of elaborate, time-consuming activities as discussion starters, leaving insufficient time for the discussion itself.

The final step in session planning is to select evaluation criteria and methods.

Reflect On and Evaluate Your Work

When educating for social responsibility, we must pause frequently to reflect on whether our educational processes are consistent with the content of the messages we want to communicate. For example, are we talking with children about social justice, respect for all beings and species, and equality, but treating some or all of them with disrespect or as our inferiors?

Educators often work under pressure or without support. Then our work becomes routine and uninspired, not challenging and dynamic. We find that our commitment and enjoyment increases dramatically when we regularly reflect on and evaluate our work. Now we try to be disciplined about it: we owe it to ourselves and the learners with whom we work to open ourselves to evaluation and reflective learning. Do you find a similar link between enjoyment of your work and the amount of energy you put into reflecting on and evaluating it?

The learning climate has a major influence on all aspects of the educational process, and evaluation is no exception. To get honest opinions from learners, they must feel relaxed and confident. But so must educators; we need to show that we are open to learning from our experiences, keen to improve, ready to grow, that we see mistakes as learning opportunities. Attitudes like these make children more likely to give reliable feedback, and may also influence them to be more reflective and open to learning from feedback.

If building and maintaining a learning climate is an important part of the educational process, then it's worth evaluating. Here's what a friend of ours, Steve Knight, did. After the orientation period for the course he was coordinating, he asked learners to fill out a detailed checklist that included items like, Do I treat you as an individual? Do I show respect for your ideas, values, and beliefs? Am I open to being challenged? Do I give each person a chance to participate? Do I show enthusiasm? Have I helped you take control of as many decisions as possible? Consider the effects it must have on the learning climate to have a facilitator who is open enough to ask these kinds of questions.

A variety of educational skills can be reflected on and evaluated. For example, we focus on our facilitation of group discussions, our use of visual and other aids, the quality of the handouts we produce, a particular session or series of sessions, and our coordination of an entire program. Here we make a few brief points about techniques we have found useful to stimulate meaningful reflection and evaluation, and to help us move the next step from reflection to new, more appropriate action.

Writing

Many educators find that writing really opens their minds (and often their hearts, too) and brings fresh insight and new motivation. Some people try to write up notes about how the session went and how they felt about it as soon as possible afterward. If there was a critical incident of some sort during a session, you could write about it to analyze what happened and get ideas about how to prevent similar problems in the future. Keep track of your feelings and insights by writing in a learning diary, or use letter writing. Sometimes we write letters intending to share our ideas, but often it is with no intention of delivering the letter.

Try writing reflective letters to colleagues, learners, parents of learners, authors, even historical figures. If you prefer poetry or other forms of written expression, experiment until you find something that serves the purposes of focusing your thoughts and opening the possibility for new insights to form or come to a higher level of consciousness so that you can act on them.

Of course the major disadvantage of written reflection is that it is time consuming. That's why discussion is more often used.

Discussion

Reflective interaction with people who challenge, confront, and clarify issues is much easier than trying to reflect in isolation. We talk to the learners themselves, their parents, colleagues at work, and our friends, relatives, or spouses. Each of these groups brings a unique perspective to reflection and evaluation.

Given time limitations, the short attention spans of children, and the fact that young children cannot yet write, a lot of evaluation happens in short, informal discussions. For example, at the end of the summer, we asked WIND-Y members to think back and say which were their favorite sessions and why. After the peace ceremonies, we asked them what the high and low points of the evenings had been and why, and what we could change or improve for the next year.

Try including learners in a brief process review at the end of a session. "Today we did something a bit unusual when . . . . How did you feel about that?" Or, if there is a behavioral problem, "Today I found it hard to concentrate when some people . . . . Was this a problem for anyone else in the group?" In these cases, we are careful to keep the discussion positive and constructive—not whiny or judgmental—and not to mention names.

Sometimes we get feedback from parents or colleagues who sat in on a session, or who mention something in an informal discussion. Often a simple comment by a parent serves to focus our attention on an issue, and we can then respond promptly. Do you ever use peer evaluation in your work? If not, is there anyone whom you respect and with whom you would be willing to open yourself in this way?

Finally, you may find it stimulating to talk about your work and your feelings, hopes, and fears with your partner, close friends, or relatives whom you trust and respect.

Visual and Other Aids

Consider using photographs, videos, and tape recordings of sessions to stimulate both yourself and learners to reflect on and evaluate aspects of a program. Other aids include drawings, cartoons, and predesigned evaluation forms that you ask learners, peers, or parents to complete. Items to evaluate your facilitation skills might include, Do I introduce the topic clearly? How effective are the questions I use to involve learners? Do I respond promptly and appropriately to nonverbal and other cues given by learners? To evaluate a specific session you could ask, Did I try to cram in too much information? Did the session flow logically from one activity to the next? Were the objectives achieved? Was the poster legible from the back of the room?

Ultimately, we would like to see many of the children with whom we work grow up into responsible, caring citizens, expressing their concerns in ways they find personally meaningful. But in the short term, we try to evaluate our programs using some of the strategies below.

- Do attendance figures at meetings indicate that the children are keen, and do they express interest in continuing as members of the group?

- Ask the children to share their reflections about their insights and learning, perhaps using techniques like creative writing, art, mime, and role-plays, as well as discussion.

- Ask older children and teens to evaluate their learning and personal growth using self-set criteria. If these criteria are identified at the start of the program, you can plan sessions to be as relevant as possible, and the subsequent evaluation will be much easier.

- Is there evidence that the children or perhaps also members of their families are becoming more critical, aware, and active about working for change as a result of their learning?

- Ask parents for feedback using evaluation forms, formal interviews, or informal discussions.

- Ask experienced and respected peers to review session objectives and plans.

- Ask critical questions about all aspects of the program, and be open to making radical changes when necessary. For example, why was it started? How is it organized and why? Do learners have enough control over the content and process? How is time allocated? Who participates? Where, when, and how often does the group meet? To what role models are the children exposed? What intended and unintended messages are being communicated?

Many educators and parents have said the same thing to us: "We are so busy, can't you give some detailed lesson plans we could look at?" The rest of this chapter includes examples of session plans we have used. They are obviously not intended to be transplanted whole. Original exercises and techniques work best, so take what sounds useful, adapt it to suit your circumstances and purposes, and ignore the rest.

ENVIRONMENTAL EDUCATION: I AM A CHILD OF THE EARTH

The theme "I am a child of the earth" works equally well with preschoolers, young children, and teens, as long as the specific objectives and activities are age appropriate. These three sessions of one hour each were originally planned for 6- to 8-year-old day campers. We have used several of the activities in other groups too, so we include suggestions for alternative activities for both younger and older children, and some evaluative comments.

Session 1. Life-giving Forests

Learning Objectives

On completion of this session, each child will be able to
1. Explain what it means to her/him to be called a "child of the earth."
2. Explain how a forest works as an interconnected system.
3. List at least four reasons why we need to preserve forests.
4. Explain the term *deforestation* and list three major effects.
5. Commit to at least five actions s/he will take to take to prevent unnecessary deforestation.

Ice Breakers

1. Clapping circle (see page 39 for details). Sitting in a circle, the children, counselors, and leaders take turns to clap three times (hands, knees, hands) and say their name.
2. Secret message (see page 41 for details and pages 41–42 for other activities that help to break the ice and introduce the theme of a session). Whisper "I am a child of the earth" into the ear of the person next to you. S/he passes on the message immediately. See if it can get round the circle without the message changing too much. Then discuss what different people mean by being a "child of the earth."

Evaluation: Both these ice breakers work well. The children especially enjoy Secret message and giggle most of the way through it. The discussion about what it means to be a child of the earth is usually very touching—even youngsters come up with points like, "I am dependent on the earth for food, water, and air," "The earth is like a mother to me—she provides for all my needs," "My job is to look after the earth like I would care for my parents when they are old," "I love the earth like I love my parents."

Song

"I Am a Child of the Earth" is our own composition, which emphasizes that we share this planet with many other species and that we owe it to all of us to save the earth (see Appendix 3 for words and music).

Evaluation: *The children love this song and often ask to sing it again and again. In small groups, we ask them each to choose their favorite animal, and they all get a chance to mention it in a verse when it is their turn going round the circle. The tune is simple and catchy, and we hope its message is being internalized. With young children we sometimes use cardboard masks of animal faces as an aid, and each child wears one while we sing appropriate words, for example, "So says the tiger," etc.*

Circle Time

1. Read *Life in the Forest* by Eileen Curran, an excellent, illustrated resource emphasizing the interconnectedness and beauty of forest life. Then give children a chance to talk about real forests they have been in while camping, hiking, picnicking, or cycling. For older children and teens, use other resources with photographs of forests, or use a large poster of a forest scene and ask members of the group to say what comes into their minds first as they look at the natural beauty. Ask what sights, sounds, sensations, tastes, smells, and emotions they associate with a forest, and compose cooperative poems (see pages 7–8) about forests and deforestation.

2. Contrast the focus on forests with a question-and-answer session about deforestation, using information from *Good Planets Are Hard To Find* by Dehr and Bazar (1989). (See examples of questions and possible answers below.) Refer to a map or globe to show where tropical rainforests are, and explain that they are being destroyed at the rate of an area the size of England every year (Dehr and Bazar, 1989:3).

Evaluation: *The children thoroughly enjoy having the book read aloud, crowding in close to point out different things to each other and telling stories about their own experiences with squirrels, etc. As a result, this part of the session takes much longer than we initially anticipated, but their enthusiasm is too good to cut them short! The question-and-answer session is successful, but needs more time. One option is not to read the whole book by Curran, but to skip some pages in order to increase time for the question-and-answer session, especially the final, action-related question.*

Questions and Answers for Deforestation Session

1. **What is a forest?** An area of trees and plants; a home and habitat for many insects and other animals.

2. **Are there more or fewer forests today than in the past?** Fewer than in the past, because the building of cities, towns, farms, dams, and highways has caused massive deforestation. Many trees have been chopped down to get wood for heating, furniture, paper making, and the construction of houses and factories.

3. **Why are forests important?** They provide a habitat for animals and insects; they turn carbon dioxide into oxygen (they have been called "lungs of the earth"); they hold the soil in place; they shelter many valuable plants; they provide us with recreational areas where we can experience a sense of unity with nature; we can harvest products like rubber, nuts, and maple syrup from trees; and when cut, they provide wood, paper, etc.

4. **What can each of us do to help save or replenish the earth's trees and forests?** Plant a tree and care for it as it grows; use less paper and recycle it; don't use paper napkins, towels, and tissues, and use cloth instead; support organizations like Greenpeace and Friends of the Earth; wrap gifts in newsprint, and send the money your family would have spent on fancy paper wrappings to an environmental group; join a local citizen's group working to save forests, create green space, and protect natural areas; prevent forest fires when camping; write to the Rainforest Action Network, 301 Broadway, Suite 28, San Francisco, CA 94133; refuse to buy furniture and other products made from tropical hardwoods; eat less red meat, because cattle grazing destroys forests; support organizations working to prevent acid rain, which destroys trees; educate your friends and relatives about these issues.

Tape

Play "Lambeth Children," on the tape Peace by Peace by Sally Rogers, a true story about children in Ontario, Canada, who saved a forest by climbing into the trees when the loggers came.

Evaluation: Very successful. Most children don't initially believe it's true. Can children like us really influence adults? Do we really have power? It leaves them with a sense of optimism and anticipation: what can we do to help the earth? We assure them that we will focus on that question more deeply in subsequent sessions.

Outdoor Game

Children cooperate to make a human sculpture of a forest. Some lie down to be grass or dead leaves (ask them to be blown in the wind to introduce movement as well); some are young trees or shrubs, sitting or kneeling (ask them to grow); some are tall trees, stretching up on tip-toes (have them be blown in a gentle wind and in a fierce storm; some can even die and fall down). Other children may want to be birds flying, squirrels hopping, or raccoons rummaging. With very young children, some dress-up options help them to get into the spirit of this exercise. An alternative exercise for teens is a music-assisted meditational session, in which they visualize themselves as beautiful, old trees in a forest, part of a balanced ecosystem, doing no harm to anything or anyone. Feel the warm sun on your leaves. Hear the birds singing. Feel the wind blowing through your branches. Then, the loud noises of heavy machinery and shouting men intrude—the loggers are here! What do you feel now, trees? Don't you wish you could run away like the forest animals?

Being a bird.

But where will they run to? Will they ever find safety without you, the trees? After the exercise, ask people to talk about how they felt, how they feel knowing that the lifestyles of people like us contribute to such destruction, and what they might do to prevent some of it in the future.

Evaluation: The human sculpture never lasts long before the whole group collapses in a heap, especially when we introduce the idea of movement. We ask the group to freeze for a few moments every now and then, as if posing for a photo. At these times, we give feedback. "Look how this tree is blowing in the wind, and I see the raccoon has run behind that tree." This encourages them and keeps the sculpture from disintegrating too quickly. They often want to do it again as well, sometimes trying out different roles. The meditational activity is a bit unconventional, and may work better later, when the group is more relaxed with you and each other. Introduce it by saying, "Let's try something a bit different, now—I'm sure you can cope with an activity that demands some imagination and openness."

Follow-up

1. Ask children to bring pressed flowers, leaves, sticks, acorns, and pine cones for a mini-forest craft activity next session.
2. Arrange a field trip to a forest, arboretum, or tree-filled park. Younger children can run, play, climb trees, do natural treasure

hunts (searching for a feather, a small leaf with smooth edges, a pine cone, etc.), or hug a tree. Older children and teens could sketch, write poetry, play musical instruments, compose songs, and commit themselves to things they can do now to ensure that their own children will one day be able to relax in a forest.

Session evaluation: Objectives 1–4 were well achieved, but time was too limited to get into a detailed discussion for objective 5. We need either to modify the objectives, run a longer session, or shorten some of the activities (e.g., don't sing the song so long, or skip some pages in the Curran book).

Session 2. Creating a Mini-forest

Session Objectives

1. To inspire interest in forest life, and to link back to the previous session about deforestation.
2. To give children a sense of accomplishment and satisfaction in a cooperative craft activity.

Circle Time

Read *Look at a Tree* by Eileen Curran, a companion book to *Life in the Forest* (see session 1 above). Beautiful illustrations and a questioning text encourage children to examine trees and the life going on in and around them in a new light. For older children and teens, use an age-appropriate resource about trees, or consider showing the National Film Board movies *Air!* (2 minutes) and *Paradise Lost* (4 minutes), and discussing reactions to the movies.

Evaluation: A somewhat less enthusiastic response than to the book Life in the Forest, *used last session. Perhaps it feels repetitious? We should use a different activity next time, perhaps a bulletin board display or poster to introduce the same concepts.*

Crafts

Cooperative creation of a mini-forest. Make precut shapes of trees, butterflies, birds, nests, squirrels, rabbits, raccoons, beehives, frogs, clouds, and rainbows (traced from *Life in the Forest* and *Look at a Tree*, if necessary), and ask children to color or paint those and then paste them onto a large cardboard backdrop, together with the sticks, leaves, flowers, and pine cones they brought. Older children could design their own shapes instead of being given cut-outs, or could design and paint a large mural. Discuss the effects on all these plants, animals, and insects of loggers suddenly coming to clearcut our forest. Can we think of clear cutting and other means of exploiting the earth, like strip mining and drag-net fishing, as forms of pollution that must be controled if the earth is to survive?

Evaluation: *With the cut-outs, children can complete a major task quickly. They enjoy choosing which trees, insects, or animals to paint, so have extras available to encourage choice. We didn't have time for children to paste up their pieces during the session, so we assembled and pasted them up afterward, and showed the completed forest at the next session. It would be better to have them paste up their own contributions, thus having some control over the final construction of the forest. Only a few children remembered to bring leaves and pine cones, but what was brought made a good addition to the final forest. Also, asking them to bring materials gave them a preview of what would be done, so they were looking forward to this session.*

Tape

Play background music with an environmental theme while children work on the forest. *Dreams That Take Flight* is a good tape, or *Songs for Gaia.* (See Appendix 1, "Songs and Music" for suggested resources.)
Evaluation: *Children enjoy humming along to the music, and seem to appreciate the effort we take to set up a tape player just for background music. Some commented that listening to good music makes them feel more creative.*

Follow-up

Ask children to discuss with their parents and siblings what their families already do and what they are planning to do to help save the earth. Remind people to think back to the first session, when we started discussing what we could do to prevent deforestation. Make notes of the family's ideas and bring them to the next session.

Session 3: We Have One Earth

Session Objectives

1. To reinforce objective 5 of the first session, What can we do to prevent deforestation?
2. To introduce the concept of the earth as a whole, interconnected system.
3. To emphasize that the earth is in danger and is also our only possible home.

Circle Time

Get feedback from the follow-up activity about family efforts to save the earth. When relevant, read extracts from *50 Simple Things You Can Do to Save the Earth* (1989, Earthworks Group) to elaborate on points raised, or refer to the "Recycle" poster to emphasize and clarify points. Suggest that they take ideas learned from others in the group back to their own families for discussion and possible implementation.

Evaluation: A very popular activity. The children enjoy discussing this with their families and sharing ideas in the group. It gives them a sense of power and control: each of us can do something as a responsible child of the earth. Ideas include eating less red meat, starting a recycling program at the office or school, refusing styrofoam packaging, and writing to politicians about pollution control.

Demonstration

Stick paper cut-outs of the continents on the outside of a large, clear glass bowl. Fill the bowl with water to represent the oceans, and simulate currents and the effects of wind on the water by stirring the water with a spoon.

Then show people in North America "polluting" the Atlantic and Pacific oceans with, say, orange juice and dried herbs like thyme. People in Japan "pollute" with strawberry juice and oregano, and those in Europe with soy sauce and cinnamon.

Observe how quickly the pollution spreads through the water. Use a world map or globe to show how all the oceans flow into and become each other. The fact that they have different names doesn't mean that they are separate!

Having pointed out the interconnectedness of the oceans, initiate a discussion with questions like the ones below. It is exactly the same with air pollution: pollutants spewed out in one area soon spread through the air to other regions. So everyone on earth is responsible to everyone else, including other species, for keeping the earth clean. Wouldn't it be great if everyone on earth kept their little corner of it clean?

Someone may suggest that we all go live on Mars or somewhere else once the earth is unliveable—a fairly common fantasy. If so, use a poster of the solar system to explain that Venus and Mercury are much too close to the sun and therefore too hot for humans to survive, and that Mars and the other planets are much too cold. Older children enjoy atmospheric and other details about the planets as well.

Evaluation: Very successful. The children really relate to the demonstration—visual impact is so powerful. They enjoy adding the pollutants to the water; they like the visual effect and feeling of power, not the idea of polluting!

The realization that we only have one planetary home, and that we had better look after it, is a major breakthrough for many children. Some of them fantasize about escaping in a big spaceship! At the same time as exploding that myth, give them a sense of control; we can and must work together to clean up the earth. Our dream must be of a cleaner, healthier earth-world, not of deserting our home to find a new planet to mistreat and abuse in turn. Often at this point, the children want to take time to write a poem or letter of protest, or to plan a park or beach clean-up day.

Questions to Ask after the Glass Bowl Demonstration

1. **If these colored liquids in the bowl were pollution in the ocean, what would happen to the plants growing there? the fish? the animals and humans that eat the fish?** We all get sick. Did you know, for example, that the bodies of dead beluga whales washed up from the St. Lawrence River are disposed of as toxic waste, because they are so contaminated by chemicals? And fishermen in many areas are advised not to eat more than one or two fish per week from certain rivers, or they'll get poisoned.

2. **Is this kind of pollution actually happening in our oceans?** Very definitely yes.

3. **What kinds of pollutants are being dumped into rivers and oceans?** Everything from dioxins and other deadly chemicals used in factories, to human wastes, pesticides (runoff from farms and sprayed lawns into lakes and rivers), balloons (which kill marine life like turtles when swallowed), six-pack rings (which get caught round the necks of marine life and birds and then act like handcuffs when another ring gets caught on a branch), plastic bags, tin cans, and massive amounts of oil (from oil spills and off-shore drilling accidents). Use locally relevant examples, and mention the names of major polluting companies, if possible.

4. **But why do people do that?** Is it possible that some people are simply ignorant about the effects of polluting? Or is it that they don't care? Of course it's cheaper to dump waste in the river or ocean than to try to reduce waste production or to dispose of it responsibly.

5. **What can people like us do to reduce or prevent this kind of pollution?** Never throw litter on the beaches; write protest letters to politicians and companies; support organizations like *Greenpeace* and *Friends of the Earth*, which work to prevent pollution; support community calls for boycotts against companies that pollute; educate our friends and relatives about this problem, so they can also take action.

Song

"One Earth" emphasizes that pollution in one place affects everyone (see Appendix 3 for words and music).

Evaluation: *The children enjoy this song very much. And while we're singing with the guitar, they almost always ask to sing "I Am a Child of the Earth" again, too.*

INTERNATIONAL EDUCATION: I AM A MEMBER OF THE WORLD FAMILY

Identifying ourselves as members of a wider, global community, with all the rights and responsibilities that come with such membership, is part of being socially responsible citizens. We have facilitated sessions around this theme in many settings and with a wide range of age groups, from preschoolers to adults. Here, we include session plans from two of these contexts. First, we outline the plan we used in a three-hour orientation session about international education for YMCA day camp counselors, who ranged in age from 13–20. Thereafter, we include plans for a series of three sessions we have facilitated (with some adaptations) with children aged 9–11 attending YMCA day camps, and with WIND-Y club members aged 5–11. Where appropriate, we also include ideas about adapting activities for both younger and older age groups.

ORIENTATION SESSION FOR DAY CAMP STAFF

A local YMCA wanted to experiment with incorporating international education into its summer day camp program, and we were asked to orientate the day camp counselors, leaders, and staff. The session was a very difficult one. The venue was a large, echoing gymnasium with buzzing fluorescent lights; the age range was 13–20 years; the group had about forty members, too many to engage everyone as actively as we would like; and the majority were interested in familiar day camp topics like sports, computers, and crafts, rather than international education. But educators face these kinds of obstacles often enough, so it may be useful to read about the difficulties we faced.

Session Objectives

1. To explain what international education involves.
2. To introduce some of the issues raised and methods used in international education with children.
3. To stimulate participants to explore international issues.

4. To encourage participants to think of ways to include international issues in their work with day campers.

Introductions

1. Thank people for coming, introduce ourselves, and review the objectives of this session.
2. Ask people if they know the names of those sitting to the left and right of them. If not, to introduce themselves to each other. (Because the group had so many participants, we decided it would be too time consuming to do an introductory exercise around the whole circle.)
3. Using a show of hands, ask people to indicate (a) who is a counselor, who is a leader, (b) who has worked as a day camp counselor or leader before, (c) who attended day camp as a camper before getting involved as leaders or counselors, (d) who was born here in Quebec, elsewhere in Canada, and in another country?

Evaluation: *Participants appreciated seeing the objectives of the session written up on newsprint. They knew where we were going together, and we could refer back to the list periodically throughout the long session. The show of hands was interesting and in no way threatening or demanding—a quick way for everyone to get an overview of each others' past experience.*

Brainstorm

What is an internationalist? What is international education?

Evaluation: *We started with the question, "What is a nationalist?" and flowed from there into "What is an internationalist?"*

We had to talk loudly above the noise of the lights and the echoes, and some participants were clearly not interested in thinking about the questions; a few tried to make jokes and otherwise distract people. The minority of interested participants suggested ideas like a citizen of the world, a member of the global community, someone interested in international issues and development, and someone interested in the Third World. We added ideas like a person concerned with peace, social justice, and equality; a person who sees the links between development, peace, justice, and the environment; and someone who consciously tries to live in a way that supports or at least will not harm other members of the international community (e.g., by buying gifts made by co-op members in poor countries, supporting consumer boycotts designed to protect the health of people in the Third World, etc.).

This last point especially sparked some soul searching among a few participants who were initially interested in the session and who were, by then, engaged and helping us to keep the peace by telling their peers to keep quiet. At the end, one of them suggested this summary: An internationalist is someone who cares.

Small Group and Plenary Task

How does the First World differ from the Third World? Divide into small working groups of three, and ask one person in each group to take notes and another to report back ideas to the large group. Allow five minutes for the small groups to brainstorm and discuss, and then get feedback from all the groups while generating a list of differences on newsprint.

Evaluation: *Dividing into small groups worked well; people seemed to feel some responsibility to come up with ideas for their group. But they needed more than twice the time we had allocated. The plenary session also took much longer than anticipated. We asked each group to report back just one idea, going round the circle again and again until everyone had said all the items on their lists. This prevents the first group from saying all their ideas, thus dominating the session and leaving others with little to add. This went well for the first fifteen minutes or so, but then some of the participants started to lose concentration. We could sense that it was time to take a break, but we pressed on to get this exercise completed first. The lists participants had made were quite comprehensive. We had a checklist prepared in advance (see below), and did not have to add many items once the group had contributed all their ideas. But fleshing out each point, however briefly, does take time. For example, we had posters from Amnesty International that we showed the group when one of them mentioned human rights abuses, or we would give statistics about infant mortality rates or adult literacy, and so on.*

Differences Between the First and Third Worlds

- Child exploitation and child labor
- Communication systems
- Education standards and facilities, and percentages of the child population in school
- Death rates, infant and child mortality rates
- Diseases
- Food
- Gap between rich and poor within communities and countries
- Health care
- Housing
- Human rights violations
- Income
- Literacy
- Migration of populations
- Nutrition

- Population growth rates
- Poverty
- Refugees
- Repression
- Sanitation
- Social problems (e.g., drug and alcohol abuse)
- Social security (e.g., unemployment insurance, pensions, workers' compensation)
- Transport
- Unemployment and underemployment
- Urbanization
- War
- Water supplies
- Women's status
- Working conditions

Break

Movie and Discussion

One of the movies we have used in our work with children is *Children, Enfants, Niños*, a very good film that shows children from all over the world doing the things that children do: being born, eating, sleeping, washing, playing, going to school, getting sick, and so on. We showed it to this group for two reasons: it would give life to some of the points raised in the previous exercise, and we could ask them to discuss how they would facilitate a discussion with day campers who had just watched the movie.

Evaluation: What a surprise! The majority insisted that they would not show this type of movie to children. They found it to be some or all of these things: boring, too long, too serious, too depressing, too scary, too outdated (some Western children are shown in clothes that are no longer in fashion!), and generally not enjoyable. They said that children come to day camp to have fun, and that especially when a movie is shown, they expect to be entertained. It was a very weak chorus of participants who tried to make points like, "But this reflects real life very accurately!" and "But if they only watch TV cartoons, how will they learn about the problems in other parts of the world?" and "Isn't it part of our job as counselors to extend their thinking and experience?" It was difficult to end this part of the session on a positive note. One of our major objectives in showing the movie had simply not been achieved, and many in the group disagreed with our assessment about what is and is not appropriate for children. The only good thing was that the whole group was participating more actively in the dis-

cussion! We concluded, "Thank you for your ideas. This has certainly been an eye-opener for us, and maybe some of you have also been stimulated to think about what your role is as a person working with young children. Obviously, we all draw our lines in different places, and it's good to draw them consciously after some critical thought."

Break

Demonstration and Discussion

To demonstrate some learning activities and methods we use with children, we asked participants to imagine themselves as young children and to act in an impromptu role-play about discrimination, play a cooperative game, listen to an alternative story about a refugee child, and sing a song about world peace.

Evaluation: *Time was running out, so the discussion about alternative methods was quite superficial. But people seemed to enjoy participating and most thought that the children would enjoy these kinds of activities—at least more so than watching a "serious" movie!*

Evaluation of the Whole Session

Ask participants to use a scale of 1–5 where 1 is very poor and 5 is excellent, to rate the extent to which each of the objectives of the session has been achieved, adding any comments or feedback they want to give.

Evaluation: *Early in the session we had noticed that many in the group had arrived with no pens or paper, so we scrapped this evaluation plan and just referred back to the newsprint list of objectives in a kind of summary ("So, we have spent some time looking at . . . and then we . . . ."). We were not comfortable asking people to show their ratings by a show of hands—it feels a bit intrusive, like voting in public. After the session, most participants applauded dutifully when we were thanked by their supervisor, then rushed out without a word or backward glance; a few hung back to thank us in person, ask a question, or add an idea. This confirmed what we had felt throughout: the majority of them were not at all interested in international education, a small minority were vaguely interested, and fewer still had any commitment to including international issues in their day camp work. We felt that we had achieved the first two session objectives quite well, but that the final two were largely unachieved. As we wrote in our notes following this difficult session, "International (and peace, environmental, development, and human rights) education is inherently political. If people are going to do it, they need (1) personal commitment, (2) confidence, and (3) resources, ideas, support, and encouragement. In the limited time available in an orientation session like this, it is probably unrealistic to hope to convert the uncommitted. But we can, to some extent at least, help people with the second and third points above."*

INTERNATIONAL SESSIONS FOR CHILDREN

All of these ideas have been used either in our work with young YMCA day campers or WIND-Y members.

Session 1. Locating Ourselves in the World

Session Objectives

1. To create an awareness of the many different countries, cultures, and languages in the world, and of the common humanity of all peoples.
2. To emphasize that each country, culture, and language is as worthy of our respect as any other.
3. To stimulate children to identify with children in other countries, and to view themselves and others as members of a single, global family.

Ice Breaker

Back-me-up is a cooperative exercise in which children form two lines sitting back-to-back, arms linked to neighbors in their line. On a signal, they try to stand up, pushing against the backs of the children in the other line (see Deacove, 1974: insert page 13). The moral is that none of us can manage without others. And that is one of the messages of today's session about people all over the world: we need each other, we depend on each other, we should help each other.

Circle Time

1. In Human Map (see pages 14–15), children take turns saying the name of any country they know; they then represent that country in the human map. Write the names of countries on masking tape stuck to their chests. In an open space, position them near children representing nearby countries, and far from those representing countries across the ocean. Point out each country on a globe or world map, and note any parts of the world that are underrepresented in the human map. If necessary, reflect on why some entire continents or subcontinents were left out. When all children are included in the map, ask them to stretch across the ocean gaps to join hands and dance and sing, "To everyone in all the world, I reach my hand, I shake their hand."
2. Show slides, photographs, or pictures of children from different countries, then discuss the similarities and differences between children in our country and others. Refer to children in the pictures by names common in that country or culture; this personalizes the exercise and makes the foreign children seem more real. Keep the tone of discussion positive and respectful. We can value and rejoice in diversity, and not be threatened by or judgmental of it. Conclude by saying that we share the world with many other children, are all

members of the global human family, should all have the same basic human rights assured, and need to look out for each other. Ask children for ideas about something positive and concrete we could do as a group to show care for children who are not being treated like full and equal members of our world family. (Alternative activity: Show the movie *Children, Enfants, Ninos,* and facilitate a discussion about the many things children in every country have in common.)

Art Activity

Draw or paint a picture to illustrate the theme, "We are all children in the world family." Pictures will be displayed at Parents' Night, and everyone who does a picture gets her or his name in a hat and a chance to win an Oxfam *Children of the World* coloring book. Play a tape like *Part of the Family* in the background while children draw.

All children are members of the global family.

Song

"Kumbaya" is an African song emphasizing that all children have similar emotions. (If you have time, teach the children the tune for Kumbaya on a recorder or xylophone, while others accompany on rhythm instruments.)

Games

Use a game, handmade toys, decorative objects, musical instruments, or traditional costumes from other countries to bring the world home to children. Refer to the world map or globe to show where the props come from, and speculate on what children in those places might be like. Encourage the children to touch and use the toys, and to examine and admire the objects. Alternative idea for young children aged 3–8: Play *Froggy, Froggy*, a game African children play. Two "frogs" stand in the middle of an imaginary river between two pieces of string or two chalk lines. Other players chant, "Froggy, Froggy, may we cross your deep and scary, great big rushing river?" Frogs say, "Only if you have the color [red, yellow, etc.]." Those with the specified color somewhere on their clothing first walk across safely, then the others try to dash across without being caught by a frog. The first two caught become the next frogs. If only one is caught, there are three frogs next time. If none is caught, the same two frogs try again. Frogs may decide we have to do strange actions or make noises instead of displaying colors (e.g., "Only if you crawl across on hands and knees").

Follow-up

1. Ask parents, friends, or neighbors to write down the word for *hello* in as many different languages as possible.
2. Choose a country you are interested in for next session's Olympic Games Party. Ask parents and others for information about manners and customs in the chosen country. How do people there greet each other? Do they shake hands, hug, rub noses, kiss? How do they show respect? Do they take their shoes off at the door? Remove their hats when greeting? Make sure that at least some Third World countries are included. Young children will also enjoy bringing dress-up clothes, but keep it simple: just a head dress and shoes, for example.

Session 2. Locating Ourselves Culturally

Session Objectives

1. To reinforce objective 1 of session 1 above.
2. To discourage ethnocentrism (i.e., viewing one's own culture as superior).

Ice Breaker

Children share their foreign words for *hello* and explain what languages they are and where those languages are spoken. Refer to a globe or map.

Craft

Ask children to write their foreign words for *hello* in bright markers on pieces of fabric and to illustrate the pieces, which will be sewn together to make an International Friendliness Flag for display on Parent's Night.

Circle Time

Read extracts from the book *People*. Point out similarities and differences between people from different parts of the world. Refer to the previous session's slide show, photos, pictures of children, or movie, and to the globe or map when appropriate.

Tape

Listen to "Everyone's Different . . . But We Like Each Other All the Same," by Judy Irwig.

Game

In Olympic Games Party, children dress up and divide into two groups. One person from each group enters an imaginary room in the center, and pretends to be the first to arrive at a party for members of the Olympic Games teams. They must greet each other and behave politely, according to the customs of their cultures. The others observe the clothes and behaviors, and try to guess which countries or cultures are represented. Use a globe or map to point out countries. Discuss the different customs; some may seem strange to us, even funny. But if you came from a place where no one ever shakes hands or where shaking hands is what you do just before a fight, wouldn't some of the things we do seem equally funny?

Follow-up

Give each child a handout with these questions to be discussed with their families: If we had to emigrate, would we prefer to move to Nigeria in Africa, El Salvador in Central America, or Italy in Europe? Why? And if climate were not a factor, would we prefer to live in Winnipeg in Manitoba or Kuujjuaq in the far north of Quebec? Why?

Session 3. Locating Ourselves in Canada

Session Objectives

1. To introduce children to aspects of Inuit (or other Native) culture.
2. To further develop children's understanding of ethnocentrism and cultural colonization as they relate to aboriginal peoples.

Ice Breaker

In small groups, say what makes Canada special in your eyes. Then get feedback and generate a complete list in the large group.

Circle Time

1. Share feedback from the follow-up activity after the previous session (Where would your family move and why?). Discuss the results of this brief survey. Did anyone choose to move to Nigeria, a very poor country, or to El Salvador, a war-torn and poor country? Or to Kuujjuaq, a remote Inuit village with high unemployment and complex social problems?
2. "Visit" an Inuit village in the Arctic using audio and visual aids. If at all possible, arrange to have an Inuk—adult or child—attend as a guest. Show slides of Inuit housing, subsistence work, clothing, artwork, and people. Play a tape of people speaking and singing Innutitut. Use a poster with a syllabic alphabet and explain how it works. Encourage children to touch and examine real objects like parkas, seal-skin boots and mittens, and ulu knives. Discuss the similarities and differences between ourselves and Inuit children, and between Inuit and children in other parts of the world we have learned about.
3. Read *A promise Is a Promise* by Munsch and Kusagak (1989), a story about Inuit children winning over evil.

Craft

A cooperative group effort: Build, draw, cut, and paste models of traditional (igloos, dog teams, etc.) and contemporary (modern houses, snowmobiles, etc.) Inuit settlements.

Simulation Game

This is suitable for older children and teens, perhaps instead of the craft activity suggested above. Native People and Newcomers, in Reverse: Ask children to imagine themselves living a normal life with their parents. Suddenly some strangers appear. The newcomers are traders, teachers, missionaries, and policemen who arrive and tell the Native people that they should stop living in heated houses; should eat raw seals, frozen fish, and other strange foods; learn a new language called Innutitut; and wear clothes made from animal skins instead of cotton, wool, and polyester. It seems as though everything the Native people had been doing was not good enough! Discuss how it feels to hear such criticism of one's culture. How does it feel to be a newcomer? What is likely to happen to the original culture if the newcomers have their way? What may happen to the people who lose their culture? Point out how Native people in North America and elsewhere have been treated historically. Is everything that the newcomers bring *good* for the Native people? On the other hand, is it necessarily bad? What do we know about Native people's struggles to maintain their identity today? How can non-Natives support these struggles?

Follow-up

For older children and teens, recommend that they see a mainstream movie or video with an alternative cultural message, like *Dances with Wolves* or *The Mission.*

Session 4. Locating Ourselves in Our Local Community

Session Objectives

1. To introduce the concepts of discrimination, stereotyping, and prejudice.
2. To encourage children to recognize sexist, racist, and other prejudiced remarks and attitudes for what they are, and to deal with them matter-of-factly.

Circle Time

Read *The Paper Bag Princess* by Munsch (1980). Discuss what we mean by stereotyping, how the story challenges our sex-role stereotypes, and the links between stereotyping, prejudice, and discrimination.

Role-plays

Divide children into small groups and ask them to share experiences of when they or people they know were discriminated against because of their culture, language, religion, skin color, or gender, or when they discriminated against someone for these reasons. Then ask each group to choose one incident to role-play in front of the other groups.

Ask questions of the audience after each play: What did you see happening? Does this happen in real life? Why? How does it feel? What could we do to change this in the future? Include some time for discussion of how we can deal with people who make sexist or racist comments or jokes in our presence. A simple retort like, "That's racist!" or "I don't like sexist jokes" is often enough to make people rethink.

Tape

Touch a Hand, Make a Friend. Children can move and dance to the words.

Planning for Parents' Night

Decide what aspects of our work to include.

Parents' Night

Final plans are negotiated with the children. Some possibilities include

- Displaying the International Friendliness Flag and artwork about children around the world. Ask a parent to draw a name out of the hat for the Oxfam coloring book, which features children from all over the world.

- Brainstorming some of the similarities and differences between children from different countries.

- Acting out a role-play about some aspect of discrimination.

- Singing some of the songs we learned.

- Human map converting into a circle of friends holding hands around the world, singing "To Everyone Around the World."

- A ceremony of lighting candles to remember all our absent friends from other countries and cultures; parents and children can join in by calling out the names of countries where they have roots or where they feel for people suffering.

PEACE EDUCATION: I WILL WORK FOR PEACE

The ideas here were used during the build-up to the Gulf War in the summer of 1990, some with 5- to 11-year-olds in the WIND-Y group and others in YMCA day camp sessions with 11- to 12-year-olds. We have assumed two-hour sessions and that members of the learning group are well known to each other initially. The climax of this theme is a peace ceremony (see "Remembering Hiroshima" in the next section). In these plans, we move from macro-level, global peace issues to personal peace, but it can be just as challenging to start with micro-level peace issues and progress to international issues later. Please see Park and Park (1990a) for examples of sessions building on each other in the latter order.

Session 1. War and Peace

Session Objectives

1. To introduce the notion that war involves conscious human choice, that it is not something "out there," inevitable, just waiting to happen.
2. To help children get in touch with their understanding of the concepts of war and peace.

Ice Breaker

Sing "I Will Not Live with Fear" (see Appendix 3 for words and music).

Circle Time

1. Composing cooperative poems about war and peace (see pages 7–8). Ask the children to close their eyes and say whatever comes to mind when they hear the word *war*. Write down everyone's ideas. When the ideas slow down, stimulate with prompts like, "What does war sound (smell, taste, look) like?" Then do the same exercise for *peace*. Tell the children that you will edit and reorder the words to make poems for the next session. (If time permits with older children and teens, ask the group to work together to finalize their poems.)

2. Current event analysis: Canada has announced that troops will be sent to the Gulf. How do people feel about that? Why? How could we show our approval or disapproval? Is it important that people like us let politicians know what we think? Why or why not? (See below for one of the letters drafted by this group after a detailed analysis of the Gulf situation.)

Evaluation: The poetry session worked very well—see pages 8–9 for details about an added bonus that came out of it, the children's realization that their culture is unduly war-oriented.

The analysis of the Gulf situation was obviously very complex, and it was initially difficult to keep the interest of the 5- and 6-year-olds in the group. But as soon as we started an impromptu human sculpture (see pages 15–16), they got much more involved. One child started the whole sculpture by kneeling down with arms raised, being a Kuwaiti oil well. They felt that Hussein would never have invaded Kuwait were it not for the oil, and the West also had oil on its mind.

The idea of writing letters to the leaders of the Canadian and U.S. governments came from one of the youngest group members, who just said, "We should write and tell them we think they're making a bad mistake." Others immediately agreed that this would be a good idea, and they started brainstorming what they wanted to say at once. We made rough notes to capture their phrasing, and helped them to order their thoughts for the final draft.

President Bush
White House
Washington, DC   17 August, 1990

Dear President Bush,

re: Iraqi Crisis

We are children aged 5-11 years attending a series of "peace camps," and today we discussed what is happening in Iraq and Kuwait. We looked at a world map, saw where these Middle East countries are, spoke about Israel, and discussed what we think might happen in the future. We felt that we should write to you urgently to ask you to change your current policy.

We think you should not send any soldiers to the Middle East. No warships, no weapons! You are just encouraging the Arabs to start a big war with you (and the other Western countries, including Canada, who are also sending troops and ships). If the West stays out, the war there would remain a small war. But if your country and others get involved, this might just lead to the Third World War. The Red Sea will be red with blood if you don't stop. Please stop the war now. We want to survive. We are only young children . . . .

Of course we disagree with what Saddam Hussein has done. We wish he would just put up a white flag and get out of Kuwait. But at the same time, we don't think that "two wrongs make a right." The United Nations (U.N.) said that we should use sanctions against Iraq. Surely it is their job to ask different countries to join a peace-keeping force to check that sanctions are applied? Why did you react so quickly on your own and go against what the U.N. suggested? Their job is to keep world peace!

We realize that Americans are going to have to make some changes in their way of life if the oil supply from the Middle East is stopped. But wouldn't it be a great thing for our environment if less oil were used? Maybe this is just what the Earth needs to let her survive! In times of war, people only get small rations. Why not use rationing now to keep PEACE?

Some of the other things we worry about are: Who is the USSR going to side with in this conflict? Don't force them to become your enemy so soon after you made friends. And will you end up using nuclear weapons if the Iraqis blow up your ships with their mines or if they use chemical weapons against you?

Please, don't start a war. Please don't shoot anyone. Please get your ships and your soldiers out of
there.

Thank you for considering our ideas and our fears.
Please respond to us as soon as you get a chance. We'll
be hoping for a peaceful solution.

Yours truly,

Jessie Milligan (9)

GORDON MILLIGAN (6) Jasmine Anderson (8)
ANDREA ANDERSON (5)

Jamie MacDonald   Amy Taylor

Break

Outdoor Game

Red Cross Rescue (see page 13).

Art Activity

Draw or paint a picture, or make a collage of either a war scene or a peace
scene or both. Alternative activities for a small group of older children
and teens: Ask two or three people to compose and edit the letter to
government leaders from the earlier part of the session. They could then
read it to the group for final approval before writing it neatly or typing
it. A subgroup of older children or teens could also be asked to edit,
compose, and illustrate the cooperatively generated poems. One or two
members interested in speech and drama could then practice reading
the poems with plenty of expression, and present them at the next
session.

Follow-up

Bring news clippings for the bulletin board about any war- and peace-related items during the week. Discuss with your families which countries are at war at the moment. If we have to choose just one word, what would we say is the most common cause of war?

Session 2. World at War

Session Objectives

1. To inform ourselves about current wars.

2. To analyze the common causes of war.

3. To think about what individuals can do to work for peace.

Ice Breakers

1. Read the cooperative poems we composed last session.

2. Repeat the song, "I Will Not Live with Fear."

Circle Time

1. Summarize what each war- and peace-related news clipping is about before pinning them in two columns on the bulletin board. Is the war or the peace side of the board better covered? Why? Ask how people like us can get peace issues into the media. One idea: Organize a local peace ceremony and invite the media to attend (see "Remembering Hiroshima" below). If children suggest this and/or like the idea, start planning a ceremony.

2. Get feedback from last week's follow-up activity about countries at war and the causes of war. Point out countries currently at war on a world map. If possible, use different colored map tacks to distinguish civil wars from wars involving two or more countries. Alternative activity for older children: Ask them to make a poster entitled "World at War," and to research where wars are currently being fought, for how long, and over which issues. Contact Project Ploughshares (see Appendix 2) for a copy of their world map showing countries at war and Canada's role in the international arms trade. Discuss what we can do about the wars. Ideas: Send relief aid, protest by writing letters to politicians and attending peace marches, educate others, and support local, national, and international peace organizations working to prevent new wars.

   Evaluation: *This was interesting. Their reasons for war included fighting evil, getting more territory or land, religion, misunderstanding, hatred, racism, and extremes of nationalism. We mentioned other ideas*

*from Huddleston's book (1988), such as extremes of wealth and pov-
erty, competitive arms races, and the domination of public affairs by
men. When we pushed people to think of one word that best explains
the cause of most wars, they were stuck. We suggested "greed" (for
land, resources, or power), and this led to a discussion about stated
versus actual motives for war, political doublespeak, etc.*

*We explained that the Gulf crisis was a case in point; many people
in the West believed that Saddam Hussein was another Hitler, but
others felt this was just a convenient excuse to get more control in the
oil-rich Persian Gulf. After all, is Hussein really the only tyrant in the
world committing atrocities against people? If not, why are we not
sending troops to any number of African, Asian, or Central and South
American countries as well? With older children and teens, these issues can be fleshed out in more detail.*

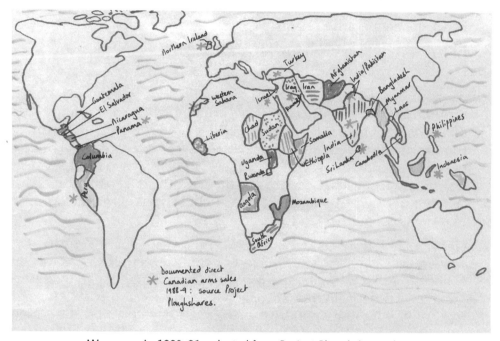

War zones in 1990–91, adapted from Project Ploughshares data.

Outdoor Games

Ask the children to make up a new game, changing the rules of a
familiar, competitive game to make it a peace-loving, cooperative game
instead. One boy thought up Peacemaker (see page 13).

Evaluation: *The group played Peacemaker with great enthusiasm.
Then Red Cross Rescue was repeated at their request as well. They
seem to enjoy these new games; they burn off energy and have fun,
and the spirit of helping and cooperation carries over into the formal
parts of the sessions as well.*

Session 3. Bringing Peace Closer to Home

Session Objective

To narrow the focus to inter- and intrapersonal peace issues.

Imaging Exercise

Play soothing, quiet, background music, and ask everyone to lie down, get comfortable, and breathe deeply for a while. Then, ask them to imagine what peace in their own hearts looks like. After a while, ask them to shift their focus to peace in their family. After the exercise, go around the circle and ask people to share as much as they want about their images.

Circle Time

1. Brainstorm a list of what causes fights in a family and allow time for children to discuss their own situations a bit, to let off steam about their siblings, and so on. Then ask, "How can each of us work to prevent at least some of the fights in our families, without becoming scapegoats for others?" Emphasize that effective peacemaking takes commitment from everyone, but that often one person can initiate the process by not being drawn into an argument. Children from dysfunctional families must never be made to feel that conflict between other members is their fault. Also explain the difference between assertiveness and aggression, perhaps by role-playing two scenes. Children could then role-play some scenes that degenerate into typical family spats, and practice alternative responses that could avoid fights in future. Peacemaking and peacekeeping are skills we all need to practice more often! With very young children, use hand puppets to act out these scenes, and ask children for ideas about how each puppet might respond more creatively and less violently to a difficult situation. Alternative activity for older children and teens: Use the question "Is conflict bad?" to start a discussion or formal debate.
2. More planning and rehearsal for the peace ceremony.

Art/Craft Activity

Make a love letter or card for the person in your family whom you fight with the most. Older children and teens might want to write poetry (see Appendix 4 for ideas) or a play about a family learning to live in peace together. Or try baking "family love cookies" or decorating plain store-bought cookies with hearts for a special family valentine night.

Follow-up

Suggest that we all make tonight a family valentine night. We could give the cards or cookies to family members, and tell them about what we had discussed and learned in the session. In families that hold regular family meetings (see Chapter 5), this could introduce a special meeting about building and keeping the peace at home.

SPECIAL EVENTS AND CEREMONIES

The session plans above relate to fairly conventional learning situations. Variety is essential, and an occasional special event remotivates children and pulls the threads of their learning together. The YMCA-day-camp parents' nights held every two weeks provided such occasions. In this section we reflect on other events that we have planned and implemented as a family, in a community setting, and in an institutional milieu.

In a Family Setting: Bringing in the New Year

We have a tradition of allowing the children to stay up as late as they like to see in the New Year. Sometimes we have taken everyone to a big party, but often we come away feeling a bit disappointed; conventional New Year celebrations in our culture may be glitzy and loud, but they are also largely hollow and superficial. So last year we had a party with ourselves as the only guests. During the day, we each worked on our projects for the party. First, we all wrote (on separate slips of paper, to be given to each other) three things that we really like or admire about every other family member. Our son spontaneously included a list *from* himself *to* himself—a great idea to boost self-esteem, which we will include in future. Because our two older children (then aged 10 and 12) were initially so appalled by the idea of actually complimenting each other in public, they stipulated the condition that all the lists would be kept anonymous; we were instructed to disguise our handwriting by writing with our left hands, and the person to whom the list was addressed would have to guess who had composed it. This worked really well. There was a wonderful atmosphere in the house all afternoon as we borrowed each others' pens and sought out special colored paper for the lists. That evening, each of us enjoyed reading aloud all the different good points others had written about us on the lists, and then guessing who had said what.

Our other task for the party was to write a list of New Year resolutions, which we would share with the family in the hope that others would then be committed to helping us live up to our resolutions during the year.

These two simple activities, after a home-cooked dinner with lots of treats, made that celebration the best yet. The children sheepishly agreed that they had really enjoyed it despite their initial resistance. For other ideas about how to build self-esteem and promote peace in a family setting, see Park and Park (1990a).

In a Community Setting: Remembering Hiroshima

For the past two years, we have helped young children to arrange and participate in neighborhood peace ceremonies to commemorate Hiroshima Day on August 6. Planning events like this involves children in detailed discussions, democratic decision making, and rehearsal; they learn about cooperation, compromise, and power sharing in the process.

Neighbors with a swimming pool agreed to let the group use their backyard for the evening ceremonies, and they opened their home to the guests for tea afterward. Invitations to community members were posted throughout the neighborhood, and families brought over extra garden chairs and snacks to share. Children's artwork was displayed on the garden fence. This small-scale and intimate approach proved very popular, even with people who were used to attending major peace ceremonies in public parks.

After welcoming everyone, we invited the president of WIND to address the group. She said she was pleased that children were being introduced to the peace movement so early, and congratulated the children on all the good work they had done throughout the summer.

Other invited guests at the ceremonies have included members of the Kids for Peace club, some Raging Grannies, and representatives from the World Conference on Religion and Peace.

A banner about low-level flights over Nitassinan was used as a discussion starter.

Activities included mimes, question-and-answer sessions to involve the adult audience and to give the children a chance to summarize and share what they had learned in the peace camps, and poetry readings. Neighbors joined in the singing of old favorites like "Where Have All the Flowers Gone?" and "Blowing in the Wind," and the children sang songs they had learned (see Appendix 3), did brief skits and role-plays, and recited a peace prayer they had composed.

The climax of the ceremony was the lighting and floating of paper lanterns the children had made, while singing a song called "Light a Candle in the Lantern" to remember the victims of Hiroshima and all wars (words and music available from CPPNW, see Appendix 2 for address). These extracts from a CPPNW information package explain the significance of lanterns in peace work.

> The peace lantern ceremony is derived from a traditional Japanese ritual in which candlelit lanterns are floated down rivers to guide ancestral souls back to the land of the dead. Some years after the bombing of Hiroshima on August 6, 1945, the traditional lantern ceremony was adapted to commemorate the victims of the first nuclear attack.
>
> It has been adapted further to represent a feeling of hope for friendship and cooperation and peace between all people throughout the world, and a determination that war, in any form, must never again be used as a method of conflict resolution.
>
> Studies have shown us that many of our children are fearful of the possibility of a nuclear war in their lifetime. In this project, we want to assure them that the responsibility for removing the threat does not rest with them only, but that they can help the many adults already working hard for peace . . . .
>
> Each year on August 6, people gather in cities all over the world—including in Hiroshima—to float lanterns to show that we also say, "Never again!"
>
> Setting one little candle afloat and seeing it drift out over the water in a swimming pool, bath tub, pond, lake, or river is like sending the light inside of us out across the world to carry our words, and to join with thousands of other lights we can't see from here. One candle doesn't do much to light up the sky, but a whole group of candles can be seen from far away, they give so much light. That's like the work of just one person. It doesn't look like much, but when it is

joined to the work of thousands of others, it can change the world . . . .

"It is better to light one candle than forever curse the darkness!" (CPPNW International Peace Lantern Exchange Project, 1989)

We notified journalists from two local newspapers before the ceremonies, and they felt that the involvement of children made the peace ceremonies sufficiently newsworthy to cover. The newspaper reports and photographs were almost as exciting for the children as the events themselves, and reached a wider audience about peace issues.

Lanterns floating on the pool.

In an Institutional Setting: Celebrating Earth Day

Recently we worked with local Brownies and Guides to celebrate Earth Day. About one hundred of them and many of their leaders and parents took part in this event in a community hall. We had previously visited and worked with one Brownie group of about fifteen girls to discuss local environmental issues, plan for Earth Day, teach songs, brainstorm for cooperative poems, and so on. Volunteer librarians set up an Earth Day display in the library and brought a selection of books about the environment to the event to encourage both adults and children to learn more about the issues, and members of the Kids for Peace and WIND-Y clubs sent artwork for display.

Brownies and Guides supporting Earth Day.

We started the event by reminding us all of the statement that had been used in the Earth Day promotional materials, "The earth's resources are borrowed from our children, not inherited from our ancestors."

Other activities included Earthy Exercises (see page 17), a participatory mime in which half the children were trees, plants, and animals in a forest and the other half were pollutants oozing, seeping, blowing, or falling in acid rain; and reading the cooperative poems about nature and pollution that the Brownies had composed.

Guest speakers, including a well-known environmental columnist and the mayor and two city councilors, talked briefly about what people in the town have done, are doing, plan to do, and should do for the earth.

They engaged the children with questions and motivated them by saying how influential children today can be. As one councilor said, he was never taught about the environment when he was young and so he had been unwittingly harming the earth. But now that he has young children who are so well informed and concerned, he has changed a lot!

We mentioned that environmentalists at last had an opportunity to congratulate the Canadian government on some positive action. The government had recently announced its Greening of the Hill program: chemical pesticides would no longer be used on the lawns on Parliament Hill, recycling was being introduced into all the offices there, and so on. We invited people to co-sign letters of congratulations we had written to the prime minister.

```
The Rt. Hon. Prime Minister
House of Commons
Ottawa, Ontario
Canada K1A  1A0
                                        20 April, 1991
Dear Mr. Mulroney,
          re: Greening the Hill

While attending an Earth Day celebration in Baie
d'Urfé today, we were told about the Federal
government's Greening the Hill program. Congratula-
tions on taking this initiative. Let's hope the
```

```
provincial  governments  and  municipalities  follow
your  lead.

Yours  sincerely,
```

Finally, we ended the event with the song "One Earth" (see Appendix 3); people spontaneously linked arms and swayed together, making this an emotionally powerful closing.

Guides, their leaders, and parents link arms for the final song.

A full-page illustrated article about the event was published in the community newsletter, and it was also covered in a newspaper article in the *Montreal Gazette*. Warm memories of the day remain, and for future Earth Day events we plan to involve Scouts, Cubs, and as many other community groups as possible. For example, art teachers can ask their pupils to paint and display natural scenes, local potters can display and sell special craft projects celebrating nature, the senior citizens' club can arrange a presentation about how the earth has been stressed during their lifetimes and say what they plan to do to help ensure its survival for their grandchildren, and so on.

The first four chapters have dealt with hands-on educational processes, on the assumption that many readers will already be working with children and youth in various situations, including schools, day camps, after-school programs, and religious organizations. If you do not yet have a forum for working, you may want to read the final chapter about organizing to educate for social responsibility in family, community, and institutional settings. We also discuss issues like how to generate and sustain enthusiasm for a program, and how to involve parents, colleagues, and others in your educational work.

Chapter 5
Getting Organized

Unless you are working in an existing organization, one of your first tasks as someone commited to education for social responsibility is to assemble a group of learners. You may be most comfortable working with a group as small and intimate as yourself, your partner, and your children. Or you may include neighbors, friends, and others in a community setting. Alternatively, you could work in a school, day camp, church, or other institutional setting where children are conveniently gathered. We discuss issues to consider in each of these situations.

WORKING WITH FAMILY MEMBERS

Issues to Consider in a Family Setting

- Is educating children for social responsibility the parents' responsibility?
- Is the nature of your home environment consistent with the values you hope to share (e.g., gender equality, nonviolence, respect, cooperation)?
- What are the characteristics of a socially responsible adult role model?
- At what age should children be formally exposed to education for social responsibility?
- What day(s) and time(s) will be suitable for family education sessions?
- What issues, topics, and themes should be included?
- Could the children's friends or extended family be included in the sessions occasionally?
- What if your spouse is reluctant to participate in the sessions?
- Will the children accept you in the role of facilitator of regular family education sessions?

Educating children for social responsibility is a fundamental part of good parenting. Of course, teachers and other adults also have a major role to play, but parents are without a doubt in the most powerful position to educate children about these issues, for two major reasons. First, we can be positive role models. If our children see us attending meetings and writing letters of protest, or hear us doing "urgent action" phone calls for a peace (or other voluntary) organization, they will know that we are concerned and active, and they are more likely to be so, too.

The second reason is that parents are usually the people with whom children form their first intimate relationships. And the nature of these earliest relationships will have a major, perhaps determining influence throughout their lives. Children who experience violence or other abuse in their families, or who live in homes where men dominate and oppress women, for example, will have trouble living in peace and partnership with others. Consider, for example, the links between Hitler's highly abused childhood—and the child-rearing practices suffered by many of his peers at the time—and the Nazi atrocities (Eisler, 1991:7).

> Women and men are the two halves of humanity. Consequently, how this relationship is structured is a fundamental model which, along with parent-child relations, profoundly affects whether all other relationships will be modeled on partnership or domination. (Eisler, 1991:2–3)

Eisler's otherwise excellent paper, "Foundations for a New World Order," has one major flaw. As a feminist, she rejects—as we emphatically do, too—calls for the return of women to their *traditional* (a code word for subservient) place. But she, like so many feminist authors, has made the error of equating "woman's traditional place"—a phrase used to refer to a *position of powerlessness* in relation to men—with a *physical place*, the family home. So while paying lip service to the fundamental role of healthy parent-child relationships, she fails to address the key issue of who is actually raising the children in modern society. There has been an effective collapse of parent-child intimacy in millions of homes around the world where both parents either choose to or have to work outside the home. Can surrogate care during a child's formative years ever replace the special closeness, bonding, and love that occur in a committed, continuous parent-child relationship? If the emergence of a new, peaceful world order at least partly depends on changing the foundations of human relations, as Eisler argues, then surely we must explore ways of supporting and affirming liberated women and men who stay home to raise their children in homes filled with love, trust, acceptance, security, consistency, fairness, cooperation, equality, respect, and peace; in homes where people speak out for these values in the world at large.

Providing a home with these qualities may be the single most effective thing we as parents can do to mold children into socially aware, responsible, justice-loving, peacemakers. People considering their parenting choices and child-rearing options may enjoy the excellent resources by Cahill (1983), Cardozo (1986), and Lowman (1984). Organizations that promote parent-child bonding, like La Leche League and Mothers Are Women (see Appendix 2), are providing an invaluable service, too.

As children get older, many concerned parents want to expose them to peace, justice, and environmental issues. Of course, potential learning moments occur throughout the day—witnessing a racial incident in the street, hearing about a schoolyard brawl, or reading a news report about deforestation—and these can be used as bases for discussion. To supplement this spontaneous but often rushed, interrupted, distracted, and therefore incomplete process, some parents structure formal learning opportunities with their families.

You can start as early as age 3 or 4 with a first child, and let younger siblings join in at their own pace. Try setting aside one evening each week as Peace (or Justice or Mother Earth) Night. Some families serve a special dinner, using a separate tablecloth and lighting a candle reserved for these nights. Depending on your family's ages and your beliefs and preferences, you could sing songs, read poetry, say prayers, read excerpts from a holy or other book, or let each member express a special wish or thought. Having set the scene, you could introduce specific learning activities, like those mentioned in Chapter 1.

Older children may initially resist a parent's suggestion about family education sessions. Offering a simple statement, like "Many families do this and I'd like us to try it for a few weeks, then we can decide whether we want to continue," along with encouragement from a spouse, can go a long way to quieting complaints. In some families, there may be a reluctant, skeptical, absent, or stressed-out spouse who doesn't participate. While we personally prefer working with both of us present, in other families—including single-parent ones, of course—the sessions may be equally enjoyable in the absence of one or the other parent. After the first few weeks, children will likely be into the routine and start looking forward to the unusual activities, discussions, learnings, and the special closeness that comes from sharing ideas, fears, and hopes together as a family. At that point, you could invite occasional guests, including friends, cousins, or neighbors, to join in the celebrations and learning sessions. It's a good way to spread peace around!

Another idea to build relationships and keep the peace in a family is to hold regular family meetings. At our first meeting, we all brainstormed ideas about the ground rules we wanted for the meetings. Examples included not making fun of what others say, allowing each other to finish our points before responding, accepting each other's feelings, and always being honest with each other. The tasks of chairing meetings and keeping minutes can be rotated. Agenda items are contributed by all, and include things like when we can get a pet, what we can do to prevent fighting between siblings, how we can wean ourselves off excessive television viewing, and which organizations we are going to donate money to this season. Occasionally, we refer back to the minutes at some later time when there is confusion, when someone has forgotten an agreement, or when we decide we want to renegotiate a family rule.

At first, our preteen children were a bit skeptical of the process and complained when we said it was time for a family meeting. We held them once a week at first; now we have democratically solved so many of the previously chronic points of friction that monthly meetings are adequate. But after a few weeks, they started looking forward to the meetings, and would suggest agenda items long before we reminded them of the upcoming meeting.

How do you, as a parent, promote peace and justice? What will your children's memories be of their early exposures to these issues? Is there more you would like to do to role-model socially responsible adulthood for your children? The resources about parenting and peacemaking by Kathy and Jim McGinnis and by Mary Joan and Jerry Park (see Appendix 1) and others associated with the Institute for Peace and Justice (see Appendix 2) are excellent, and we strongly recommend the newsletter, Parenting for Peace and Justice, published by the Institute.

WORKING IN A COMMUNITY SETTING

Issues to Consider in a Community Setting

- Is there an accessible, interested group of children to work with?
- Is there a credible organization to sponsor or support your work?
- How many members can you accommodate in a learning group?
- What age range should you accept?
- What day(s) and time(s) will be suitable for meetings?
- What issues, topics, and themes should be included?

- Should you charge a small membership fee or use other fundraising approaches?
- How can you sustain the enthusiasm of members?
- How can you involve members' families and others?

In this section we describe and reflect on a small, community-based peace education project in which we worked.

Initiation of WIND-Y

When we moved to Montreal in 1988, we lived in a neighborhood of young families; there were always children playing outside or coming to visit our baby. During the first year or so, we worked informally with a small group of children to organize events, like a May Day party in the local park to celebrate the coming of spring, a peace ceremony in a neighbor's garden to remember the victims of Hiroshima, a roadside protest to make drivers respect the speed limit on our children-filled streets, and an Earth Day celebration. The children really enjoyed planning, organizing, and participating in these events, and many of their parents did, too.

May Day celebrations: preparing to dance round the Maypole.

During our second summer there, the children wanted to form a peace club to meet regularly, and they asked us to help them organize meetings. As members of West Islanders for Nuclear Disarmament (WIND), we thought that it would provide a good umbrella for our work, and that the children would enjoy being part of a larger organization. We also felt that the parents might take the issue of peace education more seriously if we acted under the auspices of an existing, credible organization like WIND. After discussions, we prepared a pamphlet inviting children to join WIND-Y (*Y* for Youth), and made it a condition of membership that their families join WIND if they were not already members. We also charged a nominal fee of $10 per child for the summer toward the costs of buying resources, providing craft materials, and so on.

Nine children between the ages of 5 and 11 joined WIND-Y in 1990. Six were immediate neighbors of ours, and the other three had to be driven or escorted by bicycle to our home for the weekly peace camps every Friday morning of the summer vacation. The themes of the camps were

- I am a member of the world family (drawing the links between international issues and peace),

- I am a child of the earth (ecology focus), and

- Peace on earth (conflict and war, what can we do to work for peace?).

Session plans for the various themes are included in Chapter 4. Activities included singing, writing poems, educational movies, cooperative games, arts and crafts, dressing up, writing letters to politicians, and planning and preparing for a second neighborhood Peace Ceremony to remember the victims of Hiroshima and of all other wars.

Follow-up to the peace camps included a newsletter, *WIND-Y World*, produced especially for children. It was distributed to all WIND families with children and to a number of peace clubs in West Island schools. In this way, we hoped to maintain the initial enthusiasm of the children who attended the camps, to keep their parents informed and motivated to continue with peace education at home, and to involve a wider group of youth than the few who could be accommodated in the summer peace camps.

Reflections on the WIND-Y Project

Looking back, there were several factors that made the formation of WIND-Y possible. We were well known to the parents of the majority of those who joined; we had the backing of a credible, local organization; we had the help of an experienced YMCA staff person, Peggy Nickels, who recommended excellent resources; and we were offering regular, structured activities to counter the "what can we do today, Mom?" problem for parents during the long summer vacation.

The major limitation of the project, as we see it, was that the peace camps took a lot of time to prepare for, and only a small number of children benefited. However, some of the ideas we used for WIND-Y did double duty in our work at YMCA day camps, so this was not such a problem in our case. We deliberately limited membership of WIND-Y, thinking that one animator (who was also looking after our young daughter) could not relate effectively to more children. But because many families went away for a holiday or camping weekends during the vacation, some sessions only had five or six children. Next time, we would accept a larger group to allow for the occasional absences of some members.

The issue of whether or not to charge a nominal fee is a complex one. On one hand, given the shoestring budgets of most voluntary organizations, it is often necessary to raise money independently for new projects like WIND-Y. Membership fees provide a quick and simple source of funds. Also, some parents may take the project more seriously if they have invested financially in it, even to a limited extent. On the other hand, one does not want to exclude anyone who cannot afford the fee, however small. Obviously, if we are aware of interested children whose families genuinely cannot afford the costs, we will make alternative arrangements to subsidize them.

Another problem in the WIND-Y group was the relatively wide age range (from 5- to 11-year-olds). While it was often fun for the older children to help the younger ones in some way, it must also have been frustrating when certain activities were pitched either at the younger or older children. Ideally, we would like to work with more homogeneous groups of children, either aged 4–7, 8–12, 13–15, or 16 and over.

WORKING IN AN INSTITUTIONAL SETTING

Some Issues to Consider in an Institutional Setting

- How can you get children initially interested in the idea of forming a peace (or environmental, etc.) club?

- How will the club fit into the existing institutional structures?

- Whose permission and support do you need?

- How can you ensure the support of your colleagues and the children's parents?

- Will you need funding?

- If so, should you charge a small membership fee or use other fundraising approaches?

- What venue can you use for meetings?

- What day(s) and time(s) will be suitable for meetings?

- What age range should you accept?

- How many club members can you accommodate?

- How can you advertise the club to recruit new members?
- What activities will be appropriate?
- How should leadership roles in the group be allocated?

Most children spend the majority of their waking lives with other children in institutional settings, such as schools, day care centers, after-school programs, summer day camps, Sunday school groups, sports centers, Brownies, or Scouts. If you work with children in one of these settings, you are ideally placed to help them learn about peace, justice, and ecology. Children love the sense of belonging they get from membership in a club, so you may want to consider helping them form a special peace (or social justice, or environmental) club.

In the interview below, Pat Lewis—an experienced educator and school teacher—reflects on her work with the Kids for Peace club at Beacon Hill Elementary School in Beaconsfield, Montreal. She has, in her words, been "incredibly lucky," and we would add very skilled, too; she has faced almost no opposition to her work from the staff or parents. Our own experience, and that of several other educators we have spoken to, has not always been so easy, so don't despair if you face problems getting started.

How did the Kids for Peace club start?
Pat: The principal at Beacon Hill, who was very concerned about peace, invited members of the International Youth for Peace and Justice group to speak to our students in 1986. They were high school students themselves, and they made a big impression on some of our students. Shortly afterward, some of the older students got together and decided to start a peace club at the school.

How did you personally become involved?
Pat: I can hardly remember now! I guess the students needed a faculty sponsor. They must have approached the principal, and she would have raised it at a staff meeting, and I—having been active in the peace movement for many years—would have volunteered.

How many students joined the club? And what ages are most interested?
Pat: Each year we have somewhere in the region of thirty members. Previously, it was the older students who showed most interest, but this year about half of the members are in grades 1 and 2.

How do you cope with such a large group and age range?
Pat: I guess I'm used to working with a lot of children! We use a classroom for meetings, and the number of desks available is really what limits us. I must admit that having the younger members this year is a real challenge; they can't read or write, and that greatly affects the kind of work we can do together. I've really had to make big changes to

the program to incorporate them. Other clubs, like the tap dancing and chess clubs, put limits on both the size of the membership and their ages, but I don't have the heart to turn anyone away.

What if you didn't think of it as turning them away, but merely delaying their participation for a couple of years?
Pat: [sounding skeptical] Maybe . . . but what I do is divide them into small groups a lot of the time. That seems to work, having the older members help and work with the younger ones.

When does the club meet and for how long?
Pat: We meet once a week during the noon hour. The children spend the first half hour or so eating their lunch together, and then we have about an hour to get down to business. In summer, when school closes, the club doesn't meet at all.

What kinds of activities do you include?
Pat: Well, during the formal club meetings we're limited by being there, at school, and either in a classroom or outside in the school grounds. We haven't gone on any tours or visits as a whole club, though that would be great if we could arrange transport. We share newspaper clippings about relevant topics, write letters to various people including the Canadian prime minister and the U.S. president, play cooperative games, sing, write poetry, make posters, have discussions, and so on. The children designed their own letterhead and a club logo, and they have composed a special club song. Sometimes, if I have read about an art, essay, or poetry competition open to children, I tell the group about it and ask if anyone wants to enter. But of course we don't have time for all of this in each meeting! Usually we only manage a few items on the agenda. And sometimes we invite guest speakers—for example, some of the children have grandparents who were in the last war, so they come and speak about their experiences. And we've had city councillors come, and so on.

In addition to these activities with the whole club, a small group sometimes gets together outside of school hours to do something different. For example, some of us have participated in community peace marches, anti–war toys campaigns outside shops, even town council meetings, when the children got Beaconsfield declared a nuclear-free zone. Of course, for transport for these activities, we rely on the cooperation of the parents, who have been wonderful.

How is the agenda compiled?
Pat: I usually meet with either the president or the vice-president—whoever will be leading the meeting—beforehand, and we go over the minutes from the last meeting and discuss new items which should be raised. A lot of the ideas come from the children themselves, of course.

Do the children elect the office-bearers?
Pat: Yes, they hold elections each year after the club has been going for a few weeks—that way, the new members get to know each other first.

Kids for Peace members untangle themselves in a cooperative game.

They elect a president and vice-president, and a secretary to keep minutes and notes. I usually help with typing (e.g., letters, notices to parents, etc.). We don't bother with a treasurer, because there's not much in the way of money to worry about!

Do the same people get voted into office year after year?
Pat: No, we've never had the same president twice. I guess that's because most times the children vote for people who are already in grade six, and so they have left for high school the next year. Mind you, this year for the first time we had a new situation to deal with. Our secretary was voted in, and only afterward did I realize that she was one of the youngsters from the early grades—she can't write yet! So we had to elect a co-secretary to help out!

How do you advertise the club and try to recruit new members?
Pat: The club is sponsored by the Home and School Association, which publishes a newsletter about all the activities it sponsors during noon hour, so all the families get a copy of that and can consider having their children join the club. In addition, many of the teachers encourage children in their classes to join, and of course the members themselves invite their friends to join. We also have our own bulletin board in a corridor, where we display artwork and so on, so that attracts some attention to the club. When the school has an open house, we usually put on a special display in the foyer as well. Also, we had some T-shirts printed with the name of the club, and some lapel buttons, so I guess when the children wear those, that's a form of advertising.

Have you had opposition from fellow teachers or parents?
Pat: No, I don't remember any. I've been very lucky, really. Most of the teachers have had quite similar ideas to mine about peace and other issues. And if I ask for help with some activities and so on, they are really cooperative. In my case, having a principal who was supportive of a peace initiative really helped, too. I can imagine that it might be very difficult for some teachers in schools with unsupportive principals to get a peace club going. I guess in such a case it would be best to get a group of teachers behind you first, and then go to the principal with a lot of support for your idea. But an "anti" principal could cause real problems.

As for parents, I think the fact that I have always been very active in Home and School has helped to get them on-side. As I said, Home and School decided to formally sponsor the peace club. We also invite all the parents to join us for a Peace Picnic at the end of the year, where we show a video about the club and the children put on puppet plays, sing and dance, and so on. This helps to keep parents informed and enthusiastic about the club. It's also a good idea to explain what the club is about to the School Committee, and to keep the School Council informed. That way, there is less chance of people getting the wrong idea or feeling threatened, and so on.

What do you do about membership fees and fundraising?
Pat: We don't charge a membership for the club as such, although to join Home and School in the first place, a family has to pay $10. We have never had any special fundraising events either, although some of the children are talking about the club sponsoring a child in a Third World country. The school pays for duplicating, and they have been most generous with materials.

Would you start over again if you had a choice?
Pat: Oh yes, definitely! It's been so much fun. I've been a peacekeeper for many, many years; and I've always enjoyed children. Working with them about peace and issues of justice and so on gives me a real kick.

What are your two or three finest memories of the club?
Pat: I love the Peace Picnics we have with the parents and siblings each year—that's always fun. And when the club is involved in a special assembly with the whole school, for example for Remembrance Day, and when the school honored Alicia Barratt when she won first prize in a "What I would do for peace" national competition sponsored by the Canadian Federation of University Women. I was also excited when the children came to city council and did their presentation about making Beaconsfield a nuclear-free zone. Then there was the time they wrote a letter to the owners of a shopping mall, complaining about a toy tank that children put money in to ride on. We never got a reply, but in three weeks, the tank had been removed just the same! I guess there's lots of things I remember! And there are little things, too, you know; things that one child says in a meeting, or something a parent mentions.

I guess I especially enjoy it when the children are involving others—either their parents, or other children at school, or the wider community—in their work for peace. Just this week, one of the girls was on a radio show talking about the Gulf War. Publicity is so important—it's what really counts. That's why I always try to help the children improve their written and verbal expression—in poems, for example. [See Appendix 4 for some ideas about encouraging children to write poetry.] I've always been a firm believer that the pen is mightier than the sword.

GENERATING AND SUSTAINING ENTHUSIASM

If you want to start a new venture or breathe new life into an existing one, you will need to think about how to generate and sustain enthusiasm among the children with whom you work, their parents, and your colleagues. You will also need to be aware that a few adults—some of the parents and some of your colleagues, perhaps—may object to these issues being raised with children, or your colleagues may simply resist any new ideas being introduced. As with any educational innovation, we should anticipate some initial resistance by people who may be threatened by our ideas. A new program may take some time to become accepted; your credibility will grow slowly, as people see the enthusiasm of the children, as they learn more about the issues through gradual exposure to your work with the children, and as their own perceptions of the need for this kind of work change.

Motivating Children

The children with whom we have worked have almost unfailingly been excited, interested, and cooperative; generating enthusiasm initially has not been a problem. Occasionally, one child may try to attract attention by being negative about a suggested activity, for example, but others in the group usually manage to deal light-heartedly with these attempted obstructions. If you actively engage everyone from the start and involve the children in planning, implementing, and evaluating the program, they are bound to be enthusiastic. Of course, your own attitude to the process is crucial: enthusiasm is contagious!

Don't assume that toy-gun-toting children will not want to join a peace club. We have been struck by the apparent paradox that some of the young boys who seem most fixated on war play are among those most concerned and insightful about peace in the real world. Many children are uncritically submerged in a subculture of media violence and macho superheroes, and they act out what they learn without thinking and with no real malice. We try not to judge the children, and gently question the heroism of some favorite characters whose knee-jerk response to any perceived threat is brute force. If the issue of war play comes up in a group, remember that there is a difference between fantasy play and reality, and that children playing war games are often just asserting themselves to feel more in control in a world that may be frightening. Years ago, we outlawed war play in our house and garden, saying, "This is a war-toys-free zone" or "We play peacefully here." While that spared us having to watch play that offended us, it did nothing to help the children explore real-world war-and-peace issues.

The resource by Carlsson-Paige and Levin (1987) helped us respond more creatively. Now we ask questions like "Who are you fighting, and why?" and "What do you think will happen if your plane drops a bomb on those people?" Depending on the age and mood of the child, we get answers ranging from "Yikes, I never thought of that; maybe I'll quit shooting and go play something else" to "It's just a game!" To this last retort we say, "Sure, but games often mimic what adults do in real life—like when you play doctor-doctor, or play house. And that's what really upsets us: adults with real guns and bombs are really killing people, even as we speak, and what you're doing is reminding us of that. So that's why we'd rather play something peaceful."

While you have direct access to the group, it will not be too difficult to keep the children interested and motivated—at least initially. Some will drop out and move on to other areas of interest; others will take their place. But after the first flush of excitement and novelty wears off, the challenge is to sustain the children's enthusiasm. If the club only meets during the summer or once a month, enthusiasm might wane in the interim.

Here are some ideas to sustain enthusiasm between face-to-face contacts.

- Involve children in planning future sessions to increase their commitment.

- Ask them to evaluate the sessions, and then respond to any constructive criticism you receive.

- Mail a regular update note or newsletter.

- Schedule occasional meetings to keep the group semiactive between one summer and the next.

- Phone participants or their parents occasionally (e.g., to tell them about a protest they may want to attend, or to ask for feedback on the newsletter).

- Involve some of the children at other events, where they tell of their experiences as club members or display their artwork.

Another problem emerges when the same group has been meeting for largely the same purpose for many months or even years. How can you sustain enthusiasm over the long term?

These are some of our ideas; please add yours.

- Involve children in planning and implementing sessions.
- Evaluate the sessions with them and respond creatively to their feedback.
- Vary the activities as much as possible.
- Constantly introduce new materials, resources, and opportunities for members to participate actively beyond the group itself (e.g., writing for a magazine or entering a poetry competition).
- Include a major contemporary focus: what is happening today, in the news, with respect to peace and war, environmental protection, etc.
- Rotate leadership roles in the group frequently; apprentice new leaders to experienced leaders for a training period.
- Let go of more and more functions yourself as members are able to take greater initiative and responsibility.
- Constantly try to recruit new blood: this provides opportunity for experienced members to act as mentors to newcomers.

Whatever you do, some children will drift away and get involved in other things instead. Some may outgrow the group. Others may be attracted to other issues; instead of peace, they may focus on human rights or the environment, for example. Accept that this will happen, and be reassured that some of the work you have done with them—the content and the process work—can potentially lay the foundation for a lifetime of active involvement in important social issues.

Motivating Parents

> In discussions with parents, I look for common ground and emphasize our common beliefs. I try to listen carefully to their feelings rather than immediately confront their ideas. I want them to feel that I "heard" them and was willing to spend time to understand their concerns. This often leads towards a discussion of the best interests of the children we both love and are trying to serve. I clearly spell out my purposes, hoped-for end results, and my background and bias so parents know exactly what I am trying to accomplish. (Susan Mark Landis, personal communication, 1991)

Many parents—especially those who take the question of education for social responsibility seriously—will be delighted to hear that you are raising these issues with their children. They are pleased to have their educational efforts at home being complemented or extended at school or in another setting.

However, other parents may get defensive about aspects of the content you raise and may try to block your work. If the plans you have made were previously discussed and approved by the staff as a whole, or if your institution has a policy supporting or specifically recommending the kind of educational work you are doing, you will be in a stronger position. It's important to take time at the outset to convince your colleagues of the need for this kind of work, and later to keep them informed of progress and plans.

It helps to involve parents in a formal process of consultation before you initiate your program. A special workshop could be arranged through the parent-teacher association, or you could speak at a Home and School meeting. The more parents supporting you at the outset, the less likely it is that one or two vocal opponents will be able to influence the whole program. School authorities and boards are sensitive to parental disapproval, so lobby parents initially. Attitude change is a long, slow process, and a certain amount of residual resistance is almost inevitable. It's probably healthy, acting as a stimulus and challenge; keeping us alert.

Once your program is established, keep parents informed about progress and plans. Consider making presentations at meetings; have displays at events like parents' nights, open houses, and end-of-year concerts; invite parents to sit in on sessions; set up opportunities for parents to talk to each other about the program; send letters home with the children; and write regular updates in the school (or community, church, etc.) newsletter. Parents may respond positively to a suggestion that they further explore specific issues with their children at home to reinforce and support learning in the group.

Motivating Colleagues

When you first suggest introducing education for social responsibility in an institutional setting, some colleagues may strongly support you; lean on them and enlist their help shamelessly. Some may be lukewarm or disinterested; try to engage and involve them so your group of supporters grows. Yet others may frankly oppose you; try to win them over, but don't spend so much energy dealing with their negativity that you have none left to be creative.

One way to win over colleagues is to gain the principal's support. Ask her or him for a meeting to discuss your ideas. Consult often. Get resources and the names of school officials who might be helpful. Defer to her or his long experience and superior knowledge. In short, do whatever is necessary to get the person with real power on your side. But don't neglect the rest of the staff either; it may be just your luck that the principal, after having been effectively lobbied, resigns to accept a new appointment elsewhere!

> I suggest listening as a first step to encourage others to listen to us. A lot of opposition to peace education is emotional, not rational, and people need a chance to express this. Listening is also a way of modeling a new style of conflict resolution, and is a form of peace education in itself. I'm not very good at this, but it's my ideal. (Peggy Nickels, personal communication, 1991)

Some initially resistant colleagues may be won over if you consult them early, keep them well informed of your plans, and include them appropriately in the work itself. For example, ask a skeptical colleague to preview a movie with you, or to help you set up for a complex craft activity.

Anticipate the concerns of colleagues, and be prepared to listen to them and to express your own opinion. For example, recent research may support your position, or a reputable organization may be including similar educational content and processes in their programs. A well-researched argument can be very effective in a staff meeting, especially if you stay calm throughout. Try taking the words out of your critics' mouths: "Some people fear that . . . but in fact it has been shown that the opposite occurs"; or "It is a common misconception that . . . but as many authors point out. . . ." Show your colleagues that you know the usual arguments, have considered them, and have reached a conclusion based on reason and good evidence.

Another approach is to encourage neutral colleagues to work with you, and to make supportive ones even more so. How? Engage them in casual conversations in which your own enthusiasm becomes infectious. Or show them short articles that support your ideas. Ask their advice and otherwise involve them in your plans. Or point to comments made by approving parents. Peace educators often need to lobby new ideas; we almost need to launch a political campaign to have our ideas accepted in some situations. Do you have other ideas for motivating colleagues and overcoming resistance from them?

> If a colleague is completely negative I can't expect a change of heart and it often is not even worth my time trying to explain my purposes. If I can ask a favor of the person, or need help from them, they may become more tender toward my cause, or at least me. Or if I can help them with their workload, that again might help our relationship. Change takes great self-confidence (which is why I think all peace education must begin with affirmation—it takes guts to be different!), so I try to help those most negative feel good about themselves before offering them new ideas about peace in the world. (Susan Mark Landis, personal communication, 1991)

CREATING A RIPPLE EFFECT: INVOLVING OTHERS

*   *   *   *   *

Jane arrived early for the session, proudly showing a card she had illustrated with peace signs, doves, rainbows, and clouds. We had asked each person in the group to discuss with their parents and siblings how each family works for peace in their home, in the community, in the country, and in the world, and to bring in a list of their ideas. Jane's family had clearly taken the request seriously—their lists were long and creative. Jane told the group that since their family discussion, her mother was so angered by a pro-war newspaper article that she wrote a letter to the editor—the first time she had ever done so. Jane clearly felt that she was a good influence on her mother!

When the session started, we went round the circle asking each person to mention one item on their lists. This continued until no one had any further ideas to contribute. The group then split into small groups to make posters of the ideas for display at their forthcoming Peace Ceremony. They felt it would motivate family members to see their ideas displayed, and be interesting for them to see each other's ideas.

*   *   *   *   *

"Look to the children, they are the future," we say, and working directly with children does give us hope. But we cannot write off the present generation of adults; the earth-world can't wait until today's children are adults. If they are to survive until then, they need to help their parents change now. So we try to reach parents and others through our work with youngsters.

Children speak about their experiences and insights with friends, siblings, parents, and relatives, who can also be invited to participate to some extent in the program. It is sometimes hard for adults to resist the subtle and not-so-subtle pressures that a concerned and serious child exerts on a family. Enthusiastic, knowledgeable, and committed children can encourage others to think more critically about what is happening in the world, and what they personally can do to influence events in favor of peace, justice, development, and environmental protection. In these cases, your work has a ripple effect, influencing not only the children with whom you work, but their families and others with whom they interact as well. Given this potential, it's worthwhile involving others. How can this best be done?

Children Need Help Preparing for Sessions

Our work with children is more effective if we occasionally ask them to complete tasks or small projects during the time between sessions with us. For example, we might ask them to interview their grandparents about their war experiences, to do some research about where nuclear power plants have been built in their area, to collect newspaper clippings about environmental problems, or to bring in a published poem or song that relates to the theme. Not only does this kind of preparation contribute to better sessions and give the children a greater responsibility for what happens in the group, it almost inevitably involves at least some of their family members.

Send Home Mementos from the Group

Another way to involve families is to send some of the artwork, poetry, crafts, and other work done by individuals and the group home with children, where it can be worn, played with, or displayed on the fridge door or notice board. Occasional photographs of the group in action also make excellent mementos. The idea is literally to spread the word, and to have whatever happens in the peace (or other) group become *integrated* into the homes and lives of the participants.

Notices and Newsletters

You may want to send occasional update notices or letters to families about how the group is progressing, what is planned in the next several sessions, and so on. Most parents appreciate this type of written communication, if you can manage the logistics and costs involved. Alternatively, ask each child to keep a special diary for the club, and send short, handwritten notes to the parents via the diary. Many parents would be only too willing to do follow-up activities with their children, but they may need specific suggestions and resources to do this with confidence. You might try sending a magazine with an interesting article, such as *Greenpeace* or *Amnesty International Bulletin*, home with children on a rotating basis, giving each family a chance to read and discuss it (see Appendix 1 for other magazine resources). Circulating magazines is cheaper and uses less paper than photocopying articles, and parents might browse through the whole magazine and become interested enough to join an organization working for change.

A newsletter for the club involves relatively more work and money, but may be justified in your circumstances. You could include photographs and examples of the children's artwork, and provide an overview of the topics the group has been considering and some of the highlights of the program. For the WIND-Y club newsletter that we produced, we included ideas for family activities, hoping that some families would get more deeply involved in what their children were doing.

Invite People to Sessions and Special Events

In our work at YMCA day camps, parents' nights were chances for children to display their work and act, sing, and dance in public, for their families to see some of the work we had done with the children, and for skeptical colleagues to see something of the work we were doing and the children's enthusiasm for it.

On stage at a YMCA day-camp parents' night.

Siblings could be invited to join a group visit to a museum or arboretum, and whole families could join in occasional sessions or attend an end-of-season picnic or other celebration. In Chapter 4 we mentioned the peace ceremonies and Earth Day celebrations we have organized. These are ideal for involving a wider circle of families, friends, and neighbors in the work of the group, and if the event is covered in the media, a much wider audience is reached, too.

Get Help Evaluating Your Work

Phone parents or interview them informally to discuss how they feel their children are enjoying the educational sessions. This provides feedback and makes parents feel included and perhaps more invested in working with you to make a success of the program. Colleagues can also be included in evaluation, as we discussed in Chapter 4.

All these suggestions about involving others serve two purposes. First, you reach a wider audience with the message you want to communicate. And second, the participation and interest of others helps to keep the children themselves motivated.

Speaking of evaluation, please send your feedback about this book to us % the Canadian publishers:

New Society Publishers,
P.O. Box 189,
Gabriola Island, B.C.,
Canada V0R 1X0.

Appendix 1

Resources: Learning Activities, Discussion Starters, and Educational Approaches

Listed below are some of the resources we and others have found most useful in peace, environmental, international, social justice, and human rights educational work. The largest section, "Books and Booklets," is subdivided by topic for ease of reference.

BOOKS AND BOOKLETS

Educational Approaches, Discussion Starters, and Ice Breakers

Arnold, R., D. Barndt, and B. Burke. 1985. A *New Weave: Popular Education in Canada and Central America.* Toronto: Popular Educators' Exchange. Chapter 3, "Some New Designs," is especially relevant. Available from Doris Marshall Institute for Education and Action, 818 College Street #3, Toronto, Ontario, Canada M6G 1C8. Tel. (416) 538-2334.

Crone, C. D., and C. St. J. Hunter. 1980. *From the Field: Tested Participatory Activities.* New York: World Education.

Dewey, J. 1938. *Experience and Education.* New York: MacMillan. A classic whose principles have yet to be appreciated and applied, half a century later.

Faber, A., and E. Mazlish. 1980. *How to Talk So Kids Will Listen and Listen So Kids Will Talk.* New York: Avon. Intended to help parents improve their communication skills. The same principles work equally well for educators working with children and teens.

Hammond, M., and R. Collins. 1991. *Self-Directed Learning: Critical Practice.* London: Kogan Page. See Chapter 1, "Building a Cooperative Learning Climate."

Holt, J. 1970. *What Do I Do Monday?* New York: E. P. Dutton. A classic book about helping children learn starting from their own experience.

Hope, S., and A. Timmel. 1984. *Training for Transformation: Handbook for Community Workers,* books 1, 2, and 3. Gweru, Zimbabwe: Mambo.

Kendall, F. 1983. *Super Parents, Super Children.* Johannesburg, South Africa: Delta. Intended for parents, the principles apply equally to educators.

Postman, N., and C. Weingartner. 1969. *Teaching as a Subversive Activity.* Harmondsworth: Penguin.

Rogers, C. 1983. *Freedom to Learn for the 80s.* Columbus: Charles E. Merrill. Inspiring accounts by Rogers and contributing authors about how they have given children the chance to learn rather than be taught.

Werner, D., and B. Bower. 1982. *Helping Health Workers Learn.* Palo Alto, Calif.: Hesperian Foundation. Although the specific focus of this book is training village health workers, the ideas are easily adaptable and the educational principles are universal.

The Environment

Curran, E. 1985a. *Life in the Forest.* Mahwah, N.J.: Troll Associates.

———. 1985b. *Look at a Tree.* Mahwah, N.J.: Troll Associates.

Degler, T., and Pollution Probe. 1990. *The Canadian Junior Green Guide: How You Can Help Save Our World.* Toronto: McClelland and Stewart.

Dehr, R., and R. Bazar. 1989. *Good Planets Are Hard to Find! An Environmental Information Guide, Dictionary and Action Book for Kids (and Adults).* Earth Beat Press, PO Box 33852, Station D, Vancouver, BC, Canada V6J 4L6. Tel. (604) 736-6931. Packed full of accessible data and beautiful to look at. Highly recommended.

Dorfman, G., and World Wildlife Fund. 1989. *Our World in Danger.* Loughborough, U.K.: Ladybird Books. An excellent introduction to the threats facing world wildlife; suitable for young children.

Earthworks Group. 1989. *50 Simple Things You Can Do to Save the Earth.* Berkeley: Earthworks.

———. 1990. *50 Simple Things Kids Can Do to Save the Earth.* Kansas City: Earthworks.

Environment Canada. 1990. *What We Can Do for Our Environment: Hundreds of Things to Do Now.* Free copies are available from Environment Canada's Inquiry Center, 351 St. Joseph Blvd., Hull, Quebec, Canada K1A 0H3. Tel. (819) 997-2800.

Forsyth, A. 1989. *Journey Through a Tropical Rainforest.* New York: Simon and Schuster.

Grant, J. E. 1990. *The Kids' Green Plan: How to Write Your Own Plan to Save the Environment.* Markham, Ontario: Pembroke.

Harmony Foundation of Canada. 1990. *Home and Family Guide: Practical Action for the Environment.* Ottawa: Harmony Foundation.

MacEachern, D. 1990. *Save Our Planet: 750 Everyday Ways You Can Help Clean Up the Earth.* New York: Dell.

Pederson, A. 1991. *The Kids' Environment Book: What's Awry and Why.* Santa Fe, N.M.: John Muir.

Plant, J., and C. Plant. 1990. *Turtle Talk: Voices for a Sustainable Future.* Philadelphia, Gabriola Island: New Society.

Pollution Probe. 1989. *The Canadian Green Consumer Guide.* Toronto: McClelland and Stewart.

Ross, S. 1991. *What's in the Rainforest?* Enchanted Forest Press, Box 29885, Los Angeles, CA 90029, USA. An A to Z book featuring many little known creatures; beautifully illustrated.

Seed, J., J. Macy, P. Fleming, and A. Naess. 1988. *Thinking Like a Mountain: Towards a Council of All Beings.* Philadelphia, Gabriola Island: New Society.

Seuss, Dr. 1971. *The Lorax.* New York: Random House. An environmental saga by the famous children's author; also available in film or video.

Silver, D., and B. Valley. 1990. *The Young Person's Guide to Saving the Planet.* London: Virago Press.

Suzuki, D., and B. Hehner. 1989. *Looking at the Environment.* Toronto: Stoddart.

Human Rights and Social Justice

Amnesty International. 1990. *Amnesty International Annual Report.* London: Amnesty International.

———. 1991. *Human Rights Activism: An AI Info Pack for Teachers.* Ottawa: Amnesty International Canada, English section.

———. 1989. *Human Rights Education.* Revised edition. Ottawa: Amnesty International Canada, English section.

Brody, E., J. Goldspinner, K. Green, et al. 1992. *Spinning Tales, Weaving Hope: Stories of Peace, Justice and the Environment.* Philadelphia, Gabriola Island: New Society.

Cole, J. 1990. *Filtering People: Understanding and Confronting Our Prejudices.* Philadelphia, Gabriola Island: New Society.

McGinnis, J. 1989. *Helping Families Care: Practical Ideas for Intergenerational Programs.* Available from Institute for Peace and Justice (see Appendix 2 for address).

———. (ed.). 1991. *Helping Teens Care.* Available from Institute for Peace and Justice (see Appendix 2 for address).

McGinnis, K., and J. McGinnis. 1990. *Parenting for Peace and Justice: Ten Years Later.* Available from Institute for Peace and Justice (see Appendix 2 for address).

Munsch, R. M. 1980. *The Paper Bag Princess.* Toronto: Annick Press. A wonderfully humorous, antisexist story with a sting. Enjoyed by younger and older children and adults.

Slapin, B., and D. Seale (eds.). 1992. *Through Indian Eyes: The Native Experience in Children's Books.* Philadelphia, Gabriola Island: New Society.

Slapin, B., D. Seale, and R. Gonzales. 1992. *How to Tell the Difference: A Checklist for Evaluating Children's Books Featuring Native Americans.* Philadelphia, Gabriola Island: New Society.

Thomas, B., and C. Novogrodsky. 1983. *Combatting Racism in the Workplace: A Course for Workers.* Toronto: Cross Cultural Communication Center.

UNICEF. 1989. *A Children's Chorus.* New York: Penguin, E. P. Dutton. Beautifully illustrated book about the rights of the child as defined by the United Nations.

International and Development Education

Ennew, J., and B. Milne. 1990. *The Next Generation: Lives of Third World Children.* Philadelphia, Gabriola Island: New Society.

Kujundzic, C. 1988. *Children of the World: Coloring Book.* Toronto: Oxfam. Features children from many countries in everyday scenes; available from Oxfam-Canada, 175 Carlton St., Toronto, Ontario, Canada M5A 2K3.

Mabetoa, M. 1988. *A Visit to My Grandfather's Farm.* Johannesburg, South Africa: Ravan Press. A young African girl enjoys a holiday away from the city.

Munsch, R., and M. Kusagak. 1989. *A Promise Is a Promise.* Altona, Manitoba: Friesen and Sons, Annick Press. A children's story about Inuit children winning over evil.

Spier, P. 1980. *People.* New York: Doubleday.

Peace and Cooperation

Butler, S. 1986. *Noncompetitive Games.* Minneapolis: Bethany House.

Carlsson-Paige, N., and D. E. Levin. 1987. *The War Play Dilemma: Balancing Needs and Values in the Early Childhood Classroom.* New York: Teachers College Press, Columbia University.

———. 1990. *Who's Calling the Shots? How to Respond Effectively to Children's Fascination with War Play and War Toys.* Philadelphia, Gabriola Island: New Society.

Children's Creative Response to Conflict Program. 1988. *The Friendly Classroom for a Small Planet: A Handbook on Creative Approaches to Living and Problem-Solving for Children.* Philadelphia, Gabriola Island: New Society.

Cloud, K., E. Deegan, A. Evans, et al. 1984. *Watermelons Not War! A Support Book for Parenting in the Nuclear Age.* Philadelphia, Gabriola Island: New Society.

Coerr, E. 1977. *Sadako and the Thousand Paper Cranes.* New York: G. P. Putnam. A moving story of a young girl from Hiroshima who died after radiation exposure.

Condon, C., and J. McGinnis. 1988. *Helping Kids Care: Harmony Building Activities for Home, Church and School.* Available from Institute for Peace and Justice (see Appendix 2 for address).

Deacove, J. 1980. *Co-op Games Manual.* Perth: Family Pastimes (see Appendix 2 for address).

———. 1982. *Co-op Sports Manual.* Perth: Family Pastimes (see Appendix 2 for address).

———. 1987a. *Co-op Marble Games.* Perth: Family Pastimes (see Appendix 2 for address).

———. 1987b. *Co-op Parlor Games.* Perth: Family Pastimes (see Appendix 2 for address).

Faber, A., and E. Mazlish. 1987. *Siblings Without Rivalry.* New York: W. W. Norton. Excellent resource; also see other title by these authors under "Educational approaches" above.

Fletcher, R. 1986. *Teaching Peace: Skills for Living in a Global Society.* San Francisco: Harper and Row.

Glendinning, C. 1987. *Waking Up in the Nuclear Age.* Philadelphia, Gabriola Island: New Society.

Judson, S. 1984. *A Manual on Nonviolence and Children.* Philadelphia, Gabriola Island: New Society.

Kohn, A. 1986. *No Contest: The Case Against Competition.* Boston, Mass.: Houghton-Mifflin.

Kraus, R. 1976. *Boris Bad Enough.* London: Patrick Hardy Books. A delightfully illustrated story about a family of elephants learning how to live together peacefully.

Larson, J., and M. Micheels-Cyrus (eds.). 1987. *Seeds of Peace: A Catalogue of Quotations.* Philadelphia, Gabriola Island: New Society.

Leaf, M. 1977. *The Story of Ferdinand.* New York: Puffin. A charming children's book about a Spanish bull who refused to fight.

Luvmour, S., and J. Luvmour. 1990. *Everyone Wins! Cooperative Games and Activities.* Philadelphia, Gabriola Island: New Society.

Macy, J. 1983. *Despair and Personal Power in the Nuclear Age.* Philadelphia, Gabriola Island: New Society.

Maruki, T. 1980. *Hiroshima No Pika.* New York: Lothrop, Lee and Shepard. A powerfully illustrated, moving account of one family's ordeal in the days following the bomb in 1945.

McGinnis, J. 1989. *Helping Families Care: Practical Ideas for Intergenerational Programs.* Available from Institute for Peace and Justice (see Appendix 2 for address). Also see the other excellent titles by Kathy and Jim McGinnis, listed under "Human Rights and Social Justice" above.

McGinnis, K., and B. Oehlberg. 1988. *Starting Out Right: Nurturing Young Children as Peacemakers.* Available from Institute for Peace and Justice (see Appendix 2 for address).

Moore, M., and L. Olsen. 1985. *Our Future Is At Stake: A Teenagers' Guide to Stopping the Nuclear Arms Race.* Philadelphia, Gabriola Island: New Society.

Morrison, D., R. Dehr, and R. Bazar. 1985. *We Can Do It! A Peace Book for Kids of All Ages.* Namchi United Enterprises, PO Box 33852, Station D, Vancouver, BC, Canada V6J 4L6. Tel. (604) 733-4886.

Orlick, T. 1978. *The Cooperative Sports and Games Book: Challenge Without Competition.* New York: Pantheon.

Pacijou. 1987. *Cessez le Feu! Guide Pédagogique sur les Jouets Militaires.* Montreal: Fides. Available from Pacijou (see Appendix 2 for address).

———. 1989. *Imaginons des Jeux, des Jouets et des Contes pour la Paix. Fiches Pédagogiques.* Montreal: Pacijou (see Appendix 2 for address).

Quinlan, P. 1988. *Planting Seeds.* Toronto: Annick Press.

Sobel, J. 1982. *Everybody Wins.* New York: Walker and Co.

Seuss, Dr. 1984. *The Butter Battle Book.* New York: Random House.

Taafaki, I. 1986. *Thoughts: Education for Peace and One World. A Study Book for Moral Education.* Oxford: George Ronald.

Wichert, S. 1989. *Keeping the Peace: Practicing Cooperation and Conflict Resolution with Preschoolers.* Philadelphia, Gabriola Island: New Society.

MAGAZINES AND JOURNALS

Resources for Youth and Adults

Amnesty International Bulletin. Updates and analysis about human rights issues and prisoners of conscience. Available from national Amnesty International offices. In Canada, 130 Slater St., Suite 900, Ottawa, Ontario, Canada K1P 6E2.

Canadian Guider. Practical ideas for activities, reviews of resources, and an environmental column in the magazine of an organization dedicated to promoting the self-esteem of girls and women. From Girl Guides of Canada, 50 Merton Street, Toronto, Ontario, Canada M4S 1A3. Tel. (416) 487-5281.

Fellowship. Intended to "explore the power of love and truth for resolving human conflict." Available from Fellowship of Reconciliation, Box 271, Nyack, NY 10960, USA. Tel. (914) 358-4601.

Greenpeace. Environmental news and analyses. Available from national Greenpeace offices. In Canada, 2623 West Fourth Ave., Vancouver, BC, Canada V6K 1P8. Tel. (604) 736-0321.

Green Teacher. Explores environmental issues and approaches for teachers. Available from Tim Grant, 95 Robert Street, Toronto, Ontario, Canada M5S 2K5.

Holistic Education Review. See especially the Winter 1988 issue about peace education and the Fall 1989 issue about environmental education. PO Box 1476, Greenfield, MA 01302, USA.

New Internationalist. Critical analyses of current events and Third World issues. Has various national offices. In Canada, 35 Riviera Drive, Unit 17, Markham, Ontario, Canada L3R 8N4. Tel. (416) 946-0406.

Paper Crane: Canada's National Youth Peace Network Newsletter. The newsletter of Canada's National Youth Peace Network; contains updates, articles, details of competitions and tours, etc. From 555 Bloor St. West, Suite 5, Toronto, Ontario, Canada M5S 1Y6.

Parenting for Peace and Justice Newsletter. Support, resources, and inspiration for parents, from the Institute for Peace and Justice, 4144 Lindell Blvd, Rm. 122, St. Louis, MO 63108, USA. Tel. (314) 533-4445.

Sojourners: An Independent Christian Monthly. A publication from ecumenical Christians committed to a biblical vision of peace and justice. Available from Box 29272, Washington, DC 20017, USA. Tel. (202) 636-3637.

Somewhere Today. A publication about children around the world, available from Canadian International Development Agency, PO Box 1310, Postal Station B, Hull, Quebec, Canada J8X 9Z9.

Upstream Journal. Development education issues and analyses. Available from Social Justice Committee of Montreal, 1857 de Maisonneuve West, Montreal, Quebec, Canada H3H 1J9. Tel. (514) 933-6797.

Children's Magazines

Brilliant Star. A publication of the National Spiritual Assembly of the Baha'is of the USA. Intended to develop children's awareness of the oneness of humanity and to encourage spiritual awareness and development. From 4 Village Drive, Yardville, NJ 08620, USA.

Chalk Talk. Written by children, for children, ages 5–14; includes some material for parents. From 1550 Mills Rd, RR 2, Sidney, BC, Canada V8L 3S1.

Chickadee. Stories, games, and activities with an environmental focus aimed at young children, aged 3–9. Available from 56 The Esplanade, Suite 302, Toronto, Ontario, Canada M5E 1A7.

Children's Own. Written by children, for children, ages 7–12. From 747 Don Mills Rd., #106, Don Mills, Ontario, Canada. Tel. (416) 429-7204.

Hibou. French version of Owl magazine (see below). From 56 The Esplanade, Suite 302, Toronto, Ontario, Canada M5E 1A7.

Merlyn's Pen. A magazine of children's creative and prose writing and poetry. From PO Box 1058, East Greenwich, RI 02818, USA.

Owl Magazine. Stories, games, and activities with an environmental focus for children aged 8–14; from 56 The Esplanade, Suite 302, Toronto, Ontario, Canada M5E 1A7.

P3: The Earth-based Magazine for Kids. An upbeat, full-color magazine with cartoons, puzzles, data, analyses, competitions, book reviews, and an action-orientation for concerned "eco-kids." P3 stands for Planet 3—the Earth. From PO Box 52, Montgomery, VT 05470, USA. Tel. (802) 326-4669.

Sesame Street. For ages 2–6, featuring the Sesame Street characters. In Canada, from 10 Newgale Gate, Unit 4, Scarborough, Ontario, Canada M1X 9Z9. In USA, PO Box 52000, Boulder, CO 80321-2000, USA.

Skipping Stones: A Multicultural Children's Quarterly. A forum for communication among children from different countries and cultures. Encourages "cooperation, creativity, and celebration of cultural and linguistic diversity." From 80574 Hazelton Rd, Cottage Grove, OR 97424, USA. Tel. (503) 942-9434.

TOYS, GAMES, GLOBES, MAPS

Alternative toys and games are available from the gift catalogues of Amnesty International and Bridgehead (see Appendix 2 for addresses), and from the following:

Childcraft, 20 Kilmer Rd., Edison, NJ 08818, USA.

HearthSong, PO Box B, Sebastopol, CA 95473-0601.

PlayFair Toys, 1690 28th St., Boulder, CO 80301, USA.

UNICEF, 475 Oberlin Ave South, Lakewood, NJ 08701-1060.

For catalogues of co–op games, write:

Family Pastimes, RR4, Perth, Ontario, Canada K7H 3C6.

Animal Town, PO Box 2002, Santa Barbara, CA 93120, USA. Tel. (800) 445-8642.

A variety of "huggable" and inflatable globes is now available, in addition to conventional globes. The innovative Fisher-Price globe has slides of various countries built in. Available from good toy stores and educational shops.

Hug-a-planet: XTC Products, 247 Rockingstone Ave., Larchmont, NY 10538, USA. Tel. (914) 833-0200.

Inflatable Globes: General Conference of the Mennonite Church, Commission on Overseas Mission, 722 Main St., Box 347, Newton, KS 67114-0347, USA. Tel. (316) 283-5100, Fax (316) 283-1454.

Peter's Projection Map: Order from Friendship Press, PO Box 37844, Cincinnati, OH 45237, USA.

Peter's Projection Map Jigsaw Puzzle: Available from Bridgehead (see Appendix 2 for address).

SONGS AND MUSIC

Your own personal taste will probably be your best guide here. There are some excellent children's artists, such as Marlo Thomas, Red and Kathy Grammer, Raffi, Fred Penner, Sally Rogers, Sharon, Lois and Bram, Judy Irwig, and Wendy Fine, who sing about peace, global reconciliation, the environment, and interpersonal, intercultural, and international understanding. We have especially enjoyed using the *Peace Pak*, a series of three cassettes recorded in 1987 and available from Kids Records, Box 670, Station A, Toronto, Ontario, Canada M5W 1G2. *Songs for Gaia* (1990) is an excellent pack containing music and activity booklets and a cassette of environmental songs by Rosie Emery and Peter Bailey; available from The Gazette, Newspaper-in-Education, 250 St. Antoine West, Montreal, Quebec, Canada H2Y 1M6.

In addition, we have used many of the 1960s protest songs sung by artists like

Peter, Paul, and Mary, Joan Baez, Bob Dylan (e.g., "Blowing in the Wind"), and Barry McGuire ("Eve of Destruction"), as well as those by progressive singers, such as Tom Paxton, Cris Williamson, Holly Near, Ronnie Gilbert, Arlo Guthrie, and Pete Seeger, who raise issues of discrimination, exploitation, human rights violations, militarism, and environmental threats in many of their songs. Some of the old spiritual antislavery songs are also fun to sing, while raising serious issues that can be pursued in discussions. For international education sessions, we use the music and songs of different countries as discussion starters, for dancing, and during craft activities.

Please see Appendix 3 for words and music for some of the original songs we have used.

AUDIOVISUAL AIDS

Many peace, justice, and environmental organizations keep relevant films, videos, and slides, as well as printed resources. Please refer to Appendix 2 for addresses, and check with local branches, churches, and international education departments of YMCAs in your area for additional resources, like toys and handcrafts made in Third World countries.

Appendix 2

Organizations

This list of organizations in Canada and the United States includes several that are international, with offices in many countries. Depending on your location, you may have access to local citizen's groups, peace and social action committees, church, or other organizations that have the resources you need.

Amnesty International (AI)
130 Slater St., Suite 900
Ottawa, Ontario, Canada K1P 6E2
Tel. (613) 563-7214
Worldwide human rights organization working for the release of prisoners of conscience, has offices internationally. Their extensive publications inform members and supporters about international events relating to human rights abuses, and in addition they have audiovisual resource lists and gift catalogues.

Birthday Friends for Peace
PO Box 15514
Pensacola, FL 32514-5514, USA
Matches Western and Soviet students by their birthday. Send a 3 x 5 card with your name and personal information, and they will find a penpal in the Soviet Union. The service is free, but a small donation is appreciated.

Bread for the World
802 Rhode Island Ave., NE
Washington, DC 20018, USA
Resources about world hunger and poverty and hunger in the United States.

Bridgehead
487 Lewis St.
Ottawa, Ontario, Canada K2P 0T2
Markets gifts and food products from Third World countries.

Children's Campaign for Nuclear Disarmament
RD 1, Box 346
Chadds Ford, PA 19317, USA
Organizes annual letter-writing campaigns to the U.S. president.

Companeros:
Connecting U.S. and Nicaraguan Groups
5101 Waukesha Road
Bethesda, MD 20816, USA
Tel. (301) 229-7707
Resources suitable for classroom use and presenters available to discuss the program.

Council on Interracial Books for Children
1841 Broadway
New York, NY 10023, USA
Stockists of excellent books and filmstrips.

Earth Day International Secretariat
PO Box 38046
794 Fort Street
Victoria, BC, Canada V8W 3N2
Tel. (604) 743-7121
Coordinated Earth Day 1990 events internationally and will continue to do so each year. Their news updates and publications keep people informed about Earth Day activities around the world.

Educators for Social Responsibility
23 Garden St.
Cambridge, MA 02138, USA
Tel. (617) 492-1764
For excellent newsletter and curricular materials about nuclear issues and conflict resolution. They also sponsor teacher workshops.

Environmental Youth Alliance
PO Box 29031
1996 West Broadway
Vancouver, BC, Canada V6J 5C2
Tel. (604) 737-2258
An umbrella organization with which environmental groups at schools, etc. may want to link.

Family Pastimes
RR 4
Perth, Ontario, Canada K7H 3C6
Tel. (613) 267-4819
Makers and distributors of co-op board games, puzzles, and books.

Fellowship of Reconciliation
PO Box 271
Nyack, NY 10960, USA
Tel. (914) 358-4601
An "association of women and men who have joined together to explore the power of love and truth for resolving human conflict." We mentioned their publication, Fellowship, *in Appendix 1, and they also stock other useful resources. Another of their projects is Children's Creative Response to Conflict, which publishes a newsletter,* Sharing Space.

Friends of the Earth
251 Laurier Ave. W., Suite 701
Ottawa, Ontario, Canada K1P 5J6
Tel. (613) 230-3352
An international environmental lobby with groups in 36 countries. Their quarterly newsletter, Earth-Words, is an excellent resource, and they publish a variety of booklets and guides.

Greenpeace
578 Bloor St. West
Toronto, Ontario, Canada M6G 1K1
An international environmental organization with offices in many countries. Their bimonthly newsletter, Greenpeace, *is an excellent resource, and they publish booklets on many topics.*

Institute for Earth Education
PO Box 288
Warrenville, IL 60555, USA
Focused educational programs to build understanding of and harmony with the earth and its life; conducts workshops, publishes a seasonal journal and books, etc.

Institute for Peace and Justice
4144 Lindell Blvd., Rm. 122
St. Louis, MO 63108, USA
Tel. (314) 533-4445
Publishes an excellent newsletter, Parenting for Peace and Justice, *and has a variety of alternative resources available for concerned parents, teachers, counselors, etc. Write for catalogue.*

La Leche League International
PO Box 1209
Franklin Park, IL 60131-8209, USA
Has national offices worldwide, dedicated to supporting breastfeeding women. They believe that in addition to the physical health benefits, a close nursing relationship sets the foundation for strong mother-child bonding and ultimately for healthy family and social relationships.

Little Friends for Peace
4405 29th St.
Mount Rainier, MD 20712, USA
Tel. (301) 927-5474
Founders Mary Joan and Jerry Park have produced various peace resources and offer training workshops for parents and professionals and daycamps for children.

Mothers Are Women (MAW)
PO Box 4104, Station E
Ottawa, Ontario, Canada K1S 5B1
Tel. (613) 722-7851
Publish a quarterly newsletter, Homebase:
A Forum for Women at Home.

National Film Board of Canada (NFB)
Complexe Guy-Favreau
East Tower, Rm. 102
200 René-Levesque Blvd. West
Montreal, Quebec, Canada H2Z 1X4
Tel. (514) 283-4823
*Has offices and audiovisual libraries in
major cities in Canada and international
offices in New York, London, and Paris.
Many resources designed for children about
peace, the environment, internationalism,
justice, and human rights.*

Pacijou
3584 rue de Chambly
Montreal, Quebec, Canada H1W 3J9
Tel. (514) 527-2611
*A nonprofit, multidisciplinary organization
committed to the elimination of violence,
war, sexism, and racism and the promotion of peace, cooperation, ecological awareness, and human rights. Have produced a
variety of (primarily French) printed and
audiovisual resources.*

Pax Christi USA
International Catholic Peace Movement
348 E. 10th Street
Erie, PA 16503, USA
Tel. (814) 453-4955
*Publish a newsletter and stock many rele-
vant resources.*

**Peace-Justice-Service Commission,
Ohio Conference of the Mennonite
Church**
c/o Susan Mark Landis, Chairperson
11885 Keener Drive
Orrville, OH 44667, USA
Tel. (216) 683-0976
*Information about suppliers of alternative
toys and games, and resource lists. Offers
workshops for parents, churches, and educators interested in peace education.*

Peace Links
747 8th St., SE
Washington, DC 20003, USA
*Public education about peace and nuclear
issues. Information and resource kits for
parents, educators, and young people. Publishes* Student Action Update *and* Connection *newsletters; sponsors exchanges
and other programs.*

Project Ploughshares
Conrad Grebel College
Waterloo, Ontario, Canada N2L 3G6
*A project committed to ending the nuclear
arms race and conventional weapons trade.*

Rainforest Action Network
300 Broadway, Suite 28
San Francisco, California 94133, USA
Tel. (415) 398-4404
*An activist organization working on rain-
forest issues. They publish the* Rainforest
Action Network Action Alert *and the* World
Rainforest Report.

United Nations Association
300 E. 42nd Street
New York, NY 10017, USA
Tel. (212) 697-3232
*Excellent resources about global interde-
pendence.*

United States Committee for UNICEF
331 E. 38th Street
New York, NY 10016, USA
*Resources for parents and teachers about
children from around the world.*

YMCA/YWCA International Programs
*Your local YM-YWCA may have an interna-
tional programming section with resource
people and materials.*

YM-YWCA Ottawa
Children's International Centre
180 Argyle Ave.
Ottawa, Ontario, Canada K2P 1B7
Tel. (613) 237-1320, ext. 4018
*An excellent resource center for visits and
for ideas about international programming.*

Appendix 3

Songs

We wrote these songs to reinforce concepts we raise in learning sessions. As always, we encourage you to compose your own songs to meet your specific purposes.

One Earth

In this song, children like to sing the last line of each verse very loudly. For the last line of the last verse, they shout the word "die."

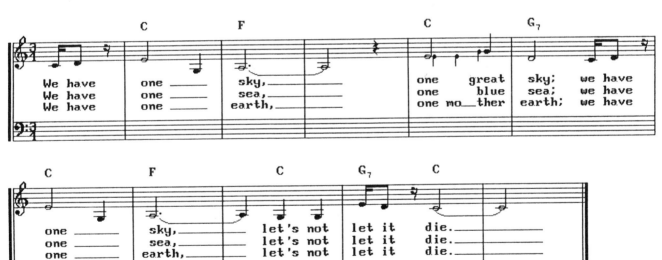

I Am a Child of the Earth

This simple and repetitive song is very popular. The tune is haunting, the words of the last lines can be changed, and the song can be sung for as long as the group cares to think of new animals and plants. Ask each person to name an animal for their own verse, and they can mime the actions of the animals too. Sing the last line—"And so say I"—loudly.

I Will Not Live with Fear

In this song, we ask children to sing softly and sway from side to side while singing the first verse of each couple. Then, for the "happy" verses, they sing loudly and clap their hands in time. The last verse is very loud and cheerful, with special emphasis on the word "work."

2- 'Cause I believe in hope,
   I believe in hope,
   I believe in hope, hope, hope,
   I believe in hope, oh, oh, oh, oh,
Oh, I believe in hope, hope, hope,
   I believe in hope, hope, hope,
   I believe in hope, hope, hope,
   I believe in hope.

3- I will not live with hate, etc.
4- 'Cause I believe in love, etc.
5- I will not live with war, etc.
6- 'Cause I believe in peace, etc.
7- And I will work for peace, etc.

Appendix 4

Experimenting with Poetry

The following are extracts and adaptations from an unpublished resource, "Variety in Verse," compiled by Pat Lewis at Beacon Hill Elementary School. The poems included were written by students aged 9–11 years who were encouraged to experiment with different forms of poetry.

HAIKU

Haiku (a poetry form with origins in Japan) do not rhyme, but have three lines with seventeen syllables altogether. The first and third lines have five syllables, and the middle line has seven.

Snowflakes drifting down;
Children play with icicles.
Nights shiver coldly.
— *Masakazu Kamoshida*

Leaves changing colors;
Scarlet, golden, deep dark red;
Days ripe with beauty.
— *Natalie Crowe*

COMPARISONS

This kind of poetry may or may not be rhymed. Often the word "like" is used. Abstract nouns may be the subject of these poems, and the five senses are often involved.

Winter is like a breath of mint;
It is as peaceful as a sleeping angora cat,
And as soft as a baby in a cradle.
— *Natalie Wagner*

DIAMANTÉ

Diamanté poems are arranged in the shape of a diamond, from which the name comes. They do not require rhyming, but there is a definite pattern to the seven lines.

Beginning with one word (a noun) and ending with a noun that is an opposite of the first, the poem develops by having a second line of two adjectives that describe the first noun. The third line of three participles again describes the first word. The middle line has two parts: the first half is made up of two nouns or adjectives again describing or renaming the first word, while the second half relates to the last word. The fifth and sixth lines also relate to the last word.

Here is an example:

Caterpillar,
Slimy, slithery,
Nesting, eating, shedding,
Green, black – – yellow, red,
Flying, gliding, hanging,
Pretty, colorful,
Butterfly.
— *Huma Saleem*

CONNECTIONS

A connection is a very precise form of poem, usually consisting of only seven words. The first and last lines are one word each, with the first being a concrete noun and the last an abstract noun with some kind of "connection" to the first. The second line is an adjective, usually telling about how the first noun may feel or smell; the third line tells how the first noun looks. The fourth line begins arbitrarily with the words "Color of . . . ." The word chosen must *not* be the name of an actual color, however. The five lines of this kind of poetry can make a very powerful impression.

Guns,
Terrifying,
Disgusting,
Color of death,
Extinction.
— *Philip LeMaistre*

Gun,
Wicked,
Cool,
Color of war,
Destruction.
— *James Ward*

FORM POEMS

These poems must be seen as well as heard. The words are put together in such a way that the words themselves form a picture of the subject of the poem. You may need to turn the page in order to read the words. The first word starts with a capital letter, and the last word is usually the noun that names the subject of the poem.

Appendix 5

Simulations and Simulation Games

Two ideas for simulations appear in Chapter 4 (see Olympic Games Party on page 72, and Native People and Newcomers, in Reverse on pages 73–74). The suggestions and statistics below are intended to stimulate your own thinking about simulations you could design to suit your own objectives and circumstances.

Some Feast While Others Starve

When dealing with issues of underdevelopment, poverty, or social injustice, you could end a session with a simulation designed to help children experience firsthand what it is like to be one of the world's dispossessed.

Just before a tea or lunch break, when everyone is hungry and thirsty, set up a barrier using a piece of string on the floor, and place a table behind it. Ask the children to sit down behind the barrier and watch while you unpack lots of fruit juice, snacks, and treats onto the table. There should be more than enough food and drinks for everyone in the group. Then, in an arbitrary way, call out the names of only a few children, no more than 15 or 20% of the group. They are welcome to cross the barrier to the table and feast. The others must stay behind the line, watching. Stop the simulation when you feel the point has been made. Then, while everyone gets a chance to eat and drink what is left, discuss what happened and relate it to the real world, using the same series of questions we recommended for decoding role-plays (see Chapter 1):

- What happened in this simulation?
- How did you feel? Did the feasters feel guilty, for example? Was it their fault that they had been "chosen" for the feast? But on the other hand, was it fair for them to ignore the hunger of those not chosen?

- Does this kind of thing happen in real life?
- Why does it happen?
- How do you feel about it?
- What can we do to change and improve the situation?

For another exercise about maldistribution of the world's resources, see "100 Hungry People" in Condon and McGinnis (1988:65–67). They describe a silent dramatization in which cereal, representing global resources, is divided into 100 cups, representing the global population. Very small amounts go to 75% of the world's population in the Third World, adequate amounts to 19% in the First and Second Worlds, and an excess goes to 6% in the United States.

Suffering Persecution for Your Beliefs

Divide the children into two groups of unequal size, and ask the smaller group to be "rulers" and the larger group to be "the people." The rulers then ask each member of "the people" a question. For very young children, try "Which color do you think is prettier—blue or green?" For older children, try something like, "Do you think Canada should have participated in the Gulf War?" This "interrogation" is done behind closed doors; no one must hear the question or the response given before it is her or his turn to be asked. Everyone who gives a "wrong" or "undesirable" answer (as arbitrarily defined by the rulers) is taken away and imprisoned, perhaps in a large cardboard box with symbolic iron bars painted on it.

Stop the simulation when you feel the point has been made, and lead a discussion using questions like:

- How did "the people" feel when they were first questioned? When they saw some people being taken away?
- How did those who were imprisoned feel? Did they know why they had been put in jail?
- How did the rulers feel, exercising that kind of power? What would they have done if the free "people" had tried to get their friends released from jail, perhaps by organizing a big demonstration outside the jail?
- Does this kind of thing happen in real life? Where? Why? What kinds of beliefs do people get persecuted for? Is it fair?
- How can this kind of injustice be opposed in the real world? What can ordinary people like us do to help those who are in prison for their beliefs?

Budgeting for War

Using pennies, nickels, and dimes to represent millions of dollars, divide up the total national budget, giving appropriately sized piles of coins to different children who are designated Ministers of Education, Health, Environment, Transport . . . and Defense. Depending on the ages of the children, you may need to spend some time discussing what each ministry is responsible for. Then, in a flight of fancy, have the Ministry of Defense dissolve itself because world peace has been assured. Let the children debate among themselves how they would divide up the money formerly used for defense (or is it offense?) between the remaining ministries. For older children, you could even ask them to prepare a speech for the next session in which each minister gets a chance to put her/his request for increased funding to parliament, and the most convincing arguments could then be rewarded with larger budgets.

These statistics, about Canada's proposed federal spending in 1991–92 on a variety of military and nonmilitary aspects of security, were provided by Project Ploughshares. All figures in billions of dollars.

Total defense budget	$13.20
Peacekeeping	*$0.35*
Transport, Coast Guard	$0.66
CSIS (Intelligence)	$0.21
Environment	
(excluding Green Plan)	$1.06
Overseas Development Aid	$3.18
Native Affairs	$2.66
External Affairs	$1.26

Here are some statistics and quotations about the international arms trade from the *New Internationalist* (no. 221, July 1991:14–17) to stimulate your thinking about other simulations you could invent.

1. The world continues to spend more on arms than it spends on anything else. In the past decade $8,000 billion was spent on arms—money that could have provided all the people in the Third World with income for three years. We spend one million million dollars on the military annually. If redirected, that money could eliminate Third World poverty. For example, a single Tornado GRI (a high-level precision bomber produced by British Aerospace) costs $40 million. The price of five of these could feed 20 million Africans for one month.

2. The cost of mounting Operation Desert Shield—not including the devastation caused by the Gulf War itself—was $53 billion. This is almost as much as the total annual foreign assistance that Third World countries get.

3. Six times as much public money in the world goes for research on weapons as for research on health protection. The Third World spends 66% more on the military than on education.

4. There is one soldier per 240 people in the Third World, one doctor per 1,950. Yet the chance of dying from social neglect, malnutrition, and preventable disease is 33 times greater than dying from war.

5. Global military spending fell by 5% in 1990 to about $950 billion. But this follows a decade of soaring spending. So although the U.S. and USSR have cut defense budgets by 6% and 10%, they are still spending 30% and 38% more than in 1980.

6. Military spending as a percentage of gross national product (GNP):

Iraq	32.0%
Israel	19.2%
USSR	11.5%
Ethiopia	8.6%
Cuba	7.4%
USA	6.7%
China	6.0%
Sudan	5.9%
UK	5.0%
Australia	2.7%
Canada	2.2%
New Zealand	2.2%

7. The global market in conventional arms stands at about $21 billion a year.

8. The Third World accounts for only 1% of arms exports, but 55% of arms imports.

9. Half a million of the world's scientists are doing research and development for the military.

10. The top exporters of conventional arms from 1985–89, in billions:

USSR	$66.2
US	$52.8
France	$15.8
UK	$7.7

11. The top importers of conventional arms from 1985–89, in billions:

India	$17.3
Iraq	$11.9
Japan	$10.5
Saudi Arabia	$8.7

Finally, some figures from a recent Project Ploughshares (see Appendix 2) fundraising letter:

1. As every second goes by, the world squanders over $30,000 on arms.

2. Canada's role in the international arms trade is considerable. Peru, Indonesia, Sri Lanka, India, Mozambique, and Turkey, for instance, are all human rights violators or countries at war, and all have received direct sales of military arms from Canada recently. Indirectly—by sales of weapons components or parts to a third country— Canadian military goods get to Iran, Iraq, Colombia, etc.

3. In 1960, 28% of independent developing countries had military governments. Today 57% do. During the same period, their armed forces doubled and military spending grew fourfold. People are hungry, ill, and unemployed because resources are used for arms and to support armies.

References

Arnold, R., D. Barndt, and B. Burke. 1985. *A New Weave: Popular Education in Canada and Central America.* Toronto: Popular Educators' Exchange.

Arnold, R., and B. Burke. 1983. *A Popular Education Handbook: An Educational Experience Taken from Central America and Adapted to the Canadian Context.* Roseneath, Ontario: Arnold and Burke.

Cahill, M. A. 1983. *The Heart Has Its Own Reasons.* Franklin Park: La Leche League International.

Canadian Physicians for the Prevention of Nuclear War. 1988. *Children and Nuclear War: Factsheet.* Ottawa: CPPNW.

Cardozo, A. R. 1986. *Sequencing: A New Solution for Women Who Want Marriage, Career, and Family.* New York: Collier Books, MacMillan Publishing.

Carlsson-Paige, N., and D. E. Levin. 1987. *The War Play Dilemma: Balancing Needs and Values in the Early Childhood Classroom.* New York: Teachers College Press, Columbia University.

Coerr, E. 1977. *Sadako and the Thousand Paper Cranes.* New York: G. P. Putnam.

Condon, C., and J. McGinnis. 1988. *Helping Kids Care: Harmony Building Activities for Home, Church and School.* St. Louis: Institute for Peace and Justice, Meyer Stone Books.

Deacove, J. 1974. *Co-op Games Manual.* Family Pastimes, RR4, Perth, Ontario, K7H 3C6, Canada.

———. 1980. *Co-op Games Manual.* Perth: Family Pastimes, RR4, Perth, Ontario, K7H 3C6, Canada.

———. 1982. *Co-op Sports Manual.* Perth: Family Pastimes, RR4, Perth, Ontario, K7H 3C6, Canada.

———. 1987a. *Co-op Marble Games.* Perth: Family Pastimes, RR4, Perth, Ontario, K7H 3C6, Canada.

———. 1987b. *Co-op Parlor Games.* Perth: Family Pastimes, RR4, Perth, Ontario, K7H 3C6, Canada.

Eisler, R. 1991. "Foundations for a New World Order." Unpublished paper.

Dewey, J. 1938. *Experience and Education.* New York: MacMillan.

Farlow, D. (ed.). 1986. *Challenging Our Assumptions: The Role of Popular Education in Promoting Health.* Proceedings of the 5th Annual Health Promotion Workshop, sponsored by the Ontario Public Health Association and the Ontario Ministry of Health.

Freire, P. 1970. *Pedagogy of the Oppressed.* New York: Herder and Herder.

Guilbert, J.-J. 1981. *Educational Handbook for Health Personnel.* Geneva: World Health Organization.

Hammond, M., and R. Collins. 1991. *Self-Directed Learning: Critical Practice.* London: Kogan Page.

Holt, J. 1970. *What Do I Do Monday?* New York: E. P. Dutton.

———. 1983. *How Children Learn.* Harmondsworth: Penguin.

Hope, S., and A. Timmel. 1984. *Training for Transformation: Handbook for Community Workers,* books 1, 2, and 3. Gweru, Zimbabwe: Mambo.

Huddleston, J. 1988. *Achieving Peace by the Year 2000.* London: OneWorld.

Kendall, F. 1983. *Super Parents, Super Children.* Johannesburg, South Africa: Delta.

Landis, S. M. 1991. Personal communication.

Larson, J., and M. Micheels-Cyrus. 1987. *Seeds of Peace: A Catalogue of Quotations.* Philadelphia, Gabriola Island: New Society.

Lowman, K. 1984. *Of Cradles and Careers.* Franklin Park: La Leche League International.

Marsolais, S. 1990. "Children of the World: International Program, Marianopolis Day Camp." Unpublished report to Montreal YMCA.

Montreal YMCA International Programs. 1985a. "Peace through Fairness: An Introduction to International Programming for Day Camps." Unpublished YMCA report.

————. 1985b. "International Theme Week: Peace through Fairness." Unpublished YMCA report.

Morrison, D., R. Dehr, and R. M. Bazar. 1985. *We Can Do It! A Peace Book for Kids of All Ages.* Namchi United Enterprises, PO Box 33852, Station D, Vancouver, BC, Canada V6J 4L6.

Munsch, R. M. 1980. *The Paper Bag Princess.* Toronto: Annick Press.

Munsch, R. M., and M. Kusagak. 1989. *A Promise Is a Promise.* Altona, Manitoba: Friesen and Sons, Annick Press.

Nickels, P. 1991. Personal communication.

Park, M. J. 1985. *Peacemaking for Little Friends: Tips, Lessons and Resources for Parents and Teachers.* Little Friends for Peace, 4405 29th Street, Mt. Rainier, MD 20712, USA.

————. 1988. *Creating a Peace Experience: Peace Camp Curriculum and Resources.* Little Friends for Peace, 4405 29th Street, Mt. Rainier, MD 20712, USA.

Park, M. J., and J. Park. 1990a. *Family Peacemaking: Playful Gatherings and Activities. Family guidebook.* Pax Christi USA, 348 East Tenth Street, Erie, PA 16503, USA.

————. 1990b. *Family Peacemaking: Playful Gatherings and Activities. Peacemakers' Notebook.* Pax Christi USA, 348 East Tenth Street, Erie, PA 16503, USA.

Parlett, M., and G. Dearden (eds.). 1977. *Introduction to Illuminative Evaluation: Studies in Higher Education.* California: Pacific Soundings.

Postman, N., and C. Weingartner. 1969. *Teaching as a Subversive Activity.* Harmondsworth: Penguin.

Rogers, C. 1961. *On Becoming a Person.* Boston: Houghton-Mifflin.

————. 1983. *Freedom to Learn for the 80s.* Columbus: Charles E. Merrill.

Werner, D., and B. Bower. 1982. *Helping Health Workers Learn.* Palo Alto, Calif.: Hesperian Foundation.

More Resources from New Society Publishers On Education And Parenting

New Society Publishers publishes books that promote fundamental social change through nonviolent action. We try to publish books which not only analyze the ills of the world but offer constructive solutions or directions or skills. For more information about these and other New Society books, or to order our books, please contact us at:

New Society Publishers
4527 Springfield Avenue
Philadelphia, PA 19143
800-333-9093

New Society Publishers
PO Box 189
Gabriola Island, BC V0R 1X0
604-247-9737

For shipping and handling, add $2.50 for the first book ordered and 75¢ for each additional book.

DUMBING US DOWN
The Hidden Curriculum of Compulsory Schooling
John Taylor Gatto

Award-winning public school teacher reveals how the very design of public schooling defeats its aims. Provocative reading for anyone interested in allowing children to develop to their fullest potential. $9.95

SPINNING TALES, WEAVING HOPE
Stories, Storytelling and Activities for Peace, Justice and the Environment
Ed Brody et al., of the Stories for World Change Network, eds.

Multicultural stories of many styles for kids of all ages, with storytelling tips and follow-up activities. Read aloud, perform, or adapt for classroom use! $22.95

THROUGH INDIAN EYES
The Native Experience in Books for Children
Beverly Slapin and Doris Seale, eds.

Confronts the impact of the stereotyping of First Nations in children's books with essays and reviews by Native peoples. *How to Tell the Difference* is an excerpt featuring a handy checklist to help identify such stereotyping. $24.95 and $7.95 respectively.

WHO'S CALLING THE SHOTS?
How to Respond Effectively to Children's Fascination with War and War Toys
Nancy Carlsson-Paige and Diane E. Levin

Renowned researchers and teachers describe how to turn scripted war play in more creative and educational directions. Designed for work with preschool and early elementary ages. Recommended in *Time, Working Mother*, and many others. How to keep from being swamped by Ninja Turtles! $12.95

DISCOVER THE WORLD
Empowering Children to Value Themselves, Others and the Earth
Susan Hopkins and Jeffry Winters, eds.

Holistic approach to integrating personal, social, cultural and environmental responsibility into the development of children from 3 to 12. Handy charts help integrate these ideas into existing lesson plans. $14.95

EVERYONE WINS
Sambhava and Josette Luvmour

Cross-referenced handbook of cooperative games for all ages and activity levels. Tremendous fun! $8.95

THE FRIENDLY CLASSROOM FOR A SMALL PLANET
A Handbook on Creative Approaches to Problem Solving for Children
Children's Creative Response to Conflict

Time-tested handbook for building self-esteem, group cooperation and conflict resolution skills in groups of children ages 6-13. $14.95

KEEPING THE PEACE
Practicing Cooperation and Conflict Resolution with Preschoolers
Susanne Wichert

Much like *The Friendly Classroom*, but for younger children, *Keeping the Peace* helps teachers and parents bolster children's self-esteem, create a cooperative learning environment and manage conflict. 26 new activities. $12.95

A MANUAL ON NONVIOLENCE AND CHILDREN
Stephanie Judson, ed.

Classic conflict resolution, esteem and cooperative games book for elementary and junior-high-aged kids. $14.95

FILTERING PEOPLE
Understanding and Confronting Our Prejudices
Jim Cole

Gentle and persuasive exploration of prejudice for teens and adults. Picture-book style. $9.95

THE NEXT GENERATION
Third World Children and the Future
Judith Ennew and Brian Milne

First-hand accounts of lives, struggles and hopes of Third World children. Something has to change! $14.95